basic
BASIC

An Introduction to Programming

DONALD M. MONRO
Imperial College of Science and Technology
London, England

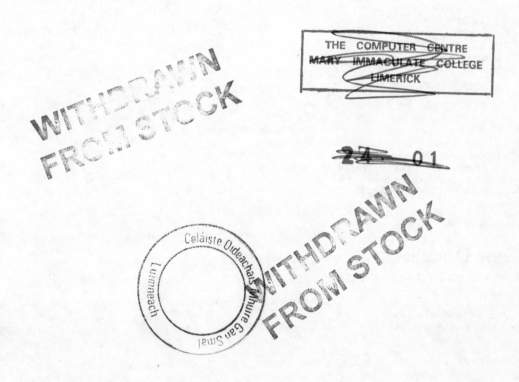
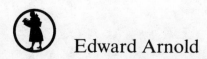 Edward Arnold

First published 1978
by Edward Arnold (Publishers) Ltd
41 Bedford Square, London WC1B 3DQ

Reprinted 1979, 1980, 1981 (twice)

BL **British Library Cataloguing in Publication Data**

Monro, Donald Martin
    Basic BASIC,
    1. Basic (Computer program language)
    I. Title
    001.6'424   QA76.73.B3

    ISBN 0-7131-2732-5

For Douglas

Printed and bound in Great Britain
at The Pitman Press, Bath

PREFACE

Computer programming is something that nearly everyone can do, and many people are now finding this out using BASIC, the language designed to help them learn. This little course gives priority to two objectives which I believe are necessary in the learning process. First of all it is fully structured, which means that I intend it to be followed in order using a computer terminal. Secondly I feel that the level of problems and examples must be neither so banal as to insult the intelligence of the reader, nor so advanced as to bewilder him. I recognize that practical computing cannot be totally non-mathematical - after all it is numbers that are dealt with - and so some of the material is related to secondary school mathematics. There are also some instances of numerical computation which I hope will be regarded from a programming point of view rather than a mathematical one. All the material is intended to be approachable.

My earlier text using the same approach at a more advanced mathematical level has been successful with students in higher education and so I have some basis for hoping that this completely new application of these ideas will meet the needs of schools and private citizens.

I have taken account of the GCE syllabus in Computing Science in choosing how much of BASIC to include, in designing the flow-charts and to some extent in choosing examples and problems. Some of the material leans gently towards the pure and applied mathematics syllabuses as well.

D.M. Monro
Totland Bay
Isle of Wight

1978

CONTENTS

INTRODUCTION

1 Computer Languages

Like any language, BASIC is used by people for the communication
of ideas. Unlike English, French, or German the intended recipient
of a communication in BASIC is a calculating machine which is some-
how equipped to accept instructions written in BASIC. There are
many computer languages, some intended for specific uses and others
which are said to be general, meaning that any computing task could
be expressed using them. BASIC is at the same time both specific
and general. The name BASIC stands for Beginners All-purpose
Symbolic Instruction Code, and the word 'beginners' is the key to
its special use as a language for learning the fundamentals of
computation in an easily understood form. At the same time BASIC is
a very useful general purpose language with some unique features.

All languages have rules of grammar, and in computing these rules
must be precise so that no statement of the language has more than
one meaning. However, BASIC has a grammar which is intentionally
simplified so that only a few simple rules must be learned before
real computations can be performed, as will be seen in Unit 1.
But because all the essential facilities for computation are present,
the emphasis can be placed on the style and methods of computation.
When the techniques of computing have been mastered it is easy to
convert to the traditional languages of large scale computation
because BASIC strongly resembles them.

2 Computer Systems

A computer system is organized around a fast and powerful
calculating machine. This machine has no personality or intelligence
of its own; anything it does is a result of human instruction. It
has a repertoire of simple orders which it obeys slavishly. A series
of these orders would be called a computer program; the concept of
a program is an easy one for humans to grasp and develops naturally
in this course by example. It is important to realize that the
machine cannot tell if its very literal interpretation of the
programmed instructions make sense. A computer's mistakes are

nearly always the fault of the program.

3 Batch and Interactive Computing

Originally computer systems were organized to deal with one program at a time, and programs were presented in groups or 'batches' which the machine processed one after the other. The programmer submitted his program to a computing service, usually on punched cards, and collected the result some time later. BASIC like any other language can be run in this way, and the majority of computing is still done in batches. The disadvantage for small programs and for learning is that the 'turnaround' time is unlikely to be less than a few hours and could be measured in days. However batch systems are very widely used particularly for production work for reasons of economy.

Interactive computing puts a programmer into direct communication with the computer, usually through a typewriter terminal. He may have the computer to himself or he may be 'timesharing' with others unseen to him. The time taken to submit a program and receive results is reduced to seconds and so program development and error correction are supported in a convenient manner. The learning process is both shortened and made more thorough because the rapid response and the straightforward nature of BASIC encourage experimentation.

4 How to Learn BASIC

First of all, it is essential to be able to run BASIC programs on a computer, ideally by using an interactive system. If only batch processing is available the course can still be followed but the ability to experiment as suggested by some exercises will be reduced. A source of expert advice is required, not so much about BASIC as about the computer system. To learn BASIC simply follow the units in order and do all the exercises because they provide exploration and clarification which are vital to complete understanding. Problems are provided at the end of each unit. Solutions to problems should be worked out on paper before trying them at a terminal. Nothing is more futile than trying to think out solutions at the keyboard; even the most tentative outline can save hours.

UNIT 1
GETTING STARTED IN BASIC

1 Introduction

An advantage of BASIC is that a small amount of information enables it to be used. This Unit introduces the simplest kind of BASIC program and shows how to create, edit, and run it.

2 A Simple Program in BASIC – the PRINT and END statements

A computer program in BASIC is a series of instructions to the computer which has a natural order and is written as statements using familiar English and mathematical terms. The meaning of the program is clear to the programmer and is also precise for the computer.

The following very simple BASIC program has two lines, each stating an instruction from the programmer to the computer:

```
1Ø PRINT 2+2
2Ø END
```

The program instructs the computer to evaluate the expression 2+2 and to print the result. Two important grammatical rules of BASIC are evident in the example:

(i)   Each of the two lines begins with a *line number*. These line numbers dictate the order of events when a program is obeyed. Every line must begin with a line number.

(ii)   The program ends with an END statement. Every BASIC program must have an END statement as its highest numbered line.

Two different statements of BASIC appear in this simple example, the PRINT statement and the END statement. The intention of the program is clear; when it is obeyed by a computer at line 10 a sum (2+2) is evaluated and printed, and at line 20 the program ends.

The meaning of complicated programs can often be clarified by the use of a flowchart, which shows diagramatically the steps

involved in a computer program and their order. This simple program
has a simple flowchart as shown in Fig. 1.1.

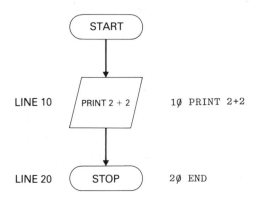

Fig. 1.1. Flowchart of a very simple BASIC program

3 Creating BASIC Programs

The creation of a program consists simply of typing into the
terminal the desired lines of BASIC each beginning with a line number.
Before this is possible the terminal must be activated and the
procedure the computer system has for recognizing permitted users
and connecting them to BASIC must be followed. This is where expert
help is required the first time.

With the computer system prepared to receive a program, the sample
program can be entered by typing it. The keyboard is laid out very
much like a typewriter but some of the special symbols such as '+'
are in unexpected places and there are some extra keys. Each separate
line is entered beginning with its line number and ending with the
'carriage return' or CR key. The first symbols typed must be the line
number but after that the number of blank spaces inserted (or left out)
is unimportant. The order in which the lines are entered is also
unimportant because the line numbers tell BASIC what the real order
should be. It is usual to separate the line numbers by 10, since
the programmer may later wish to insert extra lines, although any
separation is allowed down to consecutive numbers.

EXERCISE With the computer system ready for it, enter the sample
    program. Be careful that the first symbols in each line are the
    line number. Do not begin a line with a space, and do not attempt
    to correct errors at this stage.

4 Listing BASIC Programs – the command LIST

Typing mistakes can easily occur in entering a BASIC program, and errors in transmission between the computer and the terminal are possible. Once a program has been entered it is important to be able to examine it as it is known to the computer. The system command LIST is provided for this purpose, and causes the current version of the program to be printed on the terminal.

EXERCISE   Type in the command LIST to obtain a listing of the sample program.

It is important to distinguish between commands like LIST whose first symbol is a letter, and lines of BASIC which begin with a number.

5 Editing BASIC Programs

It is very likely that typing or other mistakes will be made when a program is entered, so that a means of editing is necessary. With BASIC it is possible to change lines, insert new lines, and eliminate unwanted ones. All these procedures are based on the line numbers; when a new line is typed in it becomes part of the program. The procedures are:

(i) To replace or correct a line: type the new line in full and 'carriage return'.

Example: The program reads

        1Ø PRANT 2+2
        2Ø END

You type in

        1Ø PRINT 2+2 and 'carriage return'

The corrected program then reads

        1Ø PRINT 2+2
        2Ø END

(ii) To insert a line: type in the new line with a suitable line number and 'carriage return'. For example a new line numbered 15 could be inserted between lines 10 and 20 of the sample program.

Example: To the sample program you add a line by typing

        15 PRINT 5+3

The program then reads

        1Ø PRINT 2+2
        15 PRINT 5+3
        2Ø END

(iii) To eliminate a line: type in only the line number, and
'carriage return'.

Example: To delete the extra line added in (ii) you type

        15   (just the line number and 'carriage return'
                        with no blank spaces)

The program then reads

        1Ø PRINT 2+2
        2Ø END

Note that to correct a line, the new version has to be typed in
full. This is sometimes tedious, so that careful original typing
is always worthwhile. Most systems also provide a means of
correcting characters in a line while it is being typed. On the
keyboard there will be a symbol which deletes the previous one - a
letter gobbling key. Usually this is a ← ('back arrow'). An
incorrect symbol in any program line or command which is noticed
before the line is finished can be removed by typing in enough
'back arrows' to reach the error, and then typing of the line can be
continued from the corrected symbol. For example the twice corrected
line

        1Ø PRA←INP 2+2←←←←←T 2+2

is the same as

        1Ø PRINT 2+2

The blank between P and 2 counts as a character.

EXERCISE Experiment with the editing facilities to add, change, and
    delete lines in the sample program. Try correcting errors while
    typing using 'back arrows'. Finally, restore the program to its
    given form and list it to be sure.

6 Running BASIC Programs – the command RUN

So far in this unit the sample program has been created, listed, and edited, but it has not been tried. The command RUN is provided to initiate the running of a program. When the RUN command is entered, the computer begins to execute the instructions given by the program. When a program is running the computer has taken control of the session and it is not possible to edit the program or to use other commands until it is finished. The sample program will terminate itself at the END statement.

EXERCISE Run the sample program, by typing in the command RUN.

7 Problems

PROBLEM 1.1 The following BASIC program has been entered. Is it correct?

        2Ø PRINP 1+3
        1Ø END

Without using the computer, follow what happens to the program as the following lines are typed in order. (CR) indicates 'carriage return'.

  (i)   3Ø END (CR)   (v)   25 PRINT 5-3 (CR)
 (ii)   1Ø (CR)   (vi)   2Ø PRIYP←←NT 1+3 (CR)
(iii)   15 (CR)   (vii)   2PR←←5 (CR)
 (iv)   2Ø PRINT 1P3 (CR)   (viii)   LIST (CR)

Is it now correct? What will happen if the RUN command is entered?

PROBLEM 1.2 Classify the following typed lines as lines of BASIC or commands according to the computer

  (i)   1Ø PRINT 3   (v)   PRINT 2+2
 (ii)   LIST   (vi)   15 LIST
(iii)   2Ø←←END   (vii)   99←←RUN
 (iv)   RUN←←←3Ø END   (viii)   LIST←←←4Ø END

Which are correct representations of the facilities described in Unit 1?

UNIT 2
THE ARITHMETIC OF BASIC

1 Introduction

Armed with the ability to prepare simple BASIC programs acquired in Unit 1, it is now possible to introduce the rules of arithmetic as they apply to BASIC. By the end of this unit it will be possible to use BASIC as a programmable calculator for the evaluation of complicated expressions.

2 Addition and Subtraction

The sample program of Unit 1 included the addition facility. An expression including addition is formed simply by placing a plus sign between the numbers to be added. In the expressions considered here the numbers are constants like, 1, 2, 3 etc., and expressions are formed from these. The program

```
1∅ PRINT 2+2
2∅ END
```

contains the *expression* 2+2 formed by the *operation* of addition between the *constants* 2 and 2. A number by itself is an expression as well, such as in

```
1∅ PRINT 35
2∅ END
```

Not surprisingly the operation of subtraction is indicated by a minus sign:

```
1∅ PRINT 4-3
2∅ END
```

Everyone knows that the order of addition is unimportant, that is, 5+1 is the same as 1+5. This is not true for subtraction as 5-1 is not the same as 1-5. This is an obvious example of a fact which will be important, namely that the order of numbers and operators like + and - in an expression is important. In BASIC operations are done from left to right, and the meaning of a program like

        1∅ PRINT 4-3+7
        2∅ END

is obvious to the programmer and the computer.

   The symbols + and - also have a meaning if they precede a number,
for example in

        1∅ PRINT -3
        2∅ END

This is not true of any other arithmetic symbols.

EXERCISE Ensure that addition and subtraction and their combination
    is understood, by trying some programs.

3 Multiplication and Division

   Multiplication in BASIC is indicated by the symbol * written
between the numbers to be multiplied. Like addition, it is of
course order-independent.

EXERCISE Try this

        1∅ PRINT 4.2*3.7
        2∅ END

Here there are *constants* which have decimal points in them. This
is always acceptable in BASIC.

   In BASIC division occurs when the symbol / is used. Division is
order-dependent so that

                    6/3 is 2
            and   3/6 is 0.5

EXERCISE Try some divisions. What does BASIC do about decimal
    points when the result of an integer division is not an integer?
    What if it is?

EXERCISE Now mix multiplication with division. Do not include
    addition or subtraction yet.

4 Exponentation

There is one more operation of arithmetic in BASIC, which is the raising of a number to a power. The vertical arrow ↑ is used as the symbol for this, not to be confused with the 'back arrow' used in editing. This is another order-dependent operation so that

$$5↑3 \text{ means } 125$$
$$\text{and} \quad 3↑5 \text{ means } 243$$

It is worth noting that fractional powers have their usual meaning,

$$2↑0.5 \text{ means } \sqrt{2} \text{ which is } 1.4142...$$

EXERCISE   Try out exponentiation, still without mixing in other operations.

5 Expressions

The introduction of more general expressions has been delayed because there is a potential ambiguity in their meaning. For example does

$$3+4*5 \text{ mean } (3+4)*5 = 35$$
$$\text{or} \quad 3+(4*5) = 23 \text{ ?}$$

It may come as a surprise that the correct result is 23, in apparent contradiction to the statement that expressions are evaluated from left to right.

6 Rules of Arithmetic in BASIC

In BASIC the rules of arithmetic are expressed in terms of a hierarchy of operations in which operations of high priority are performed before those of low priority. The order is

( )	quantities in brackets	high
↑	exponentiation	
* /	multiplication and division	
+ −	addition and subtraction	low

Hence in the expression 3+4*5, multiplication has a higher priority than addition so the meaning is 3+(4*5). Where priorities are equal, expressions are evaluated from left to right. No two operators may appear in sequence so that 1+−2 is not allowed,

although 1+(-2) is permitted because any self-contained expression
can be preceded by a + or -.   Therefore -3 is a meaningful expression
on its own but *3 is not.

In BASIC the operation of multiplication must always be stated
with a *, i.e. as 3*4. The expression (3)(4) which in normal
mathematical notation implies a multiplication is incorrect in BASIC.

The availability of brackets provides a convenient means of
changing or specifying the meaning of an expression because
expressions within brackets are evaluated before the bracketed
quantity is itself used.

EXERCISE Experiment with the meaning of the following and other
    expressions using BASIC.   Clarify them with brackets, and change
    their meaning.

$$4+5/7 \quad 7/4*2/5 \quad 3\uparrow4\uparrow5 \quad 1+2\uparrow3*4/5+6$$

7 Problems

PROBLEM 2.1   Classify as true or false

(i)	3*4↑2	is	144	(vii)	7/3+4	is	1
(ii)	3+4↑2	is	19	(viii)	4+5*3	is	19
(iii)	2+4/2	is	3	(ix)	3↑2*2	is	18
(iv)	2↑3+4	is	128	(x)	3/6/2	is	1
(v)	2↑2↑3	is	128	(xi)	2↑3↑2	is	64
(vi)	3*4+5	is	27	(xii)	9/3+2	is	5

PROBLEM 2.2   State whether the meaning changes if the brackets are
    removed.

(i)	(3*4)↑5	(v)	2↑(3+4)
(ii)	(3↑4)*5	(vi)	2+(3↑4)
(iii)	2+(3*6)	(vii)	(2↑3)+4
(iv)	2*(3+6)	(viii)	(2+3)↑4

PROBLEM 2.3   James Hunt completes 63.41 miles in 17 minutes 14.679
    seconds.   Doing all the calculations in BASIC, find his average
    speed.

PROBLEM 2.4 Freddie deposited £1 in the Incredible Building Society
    9 years and one day ago.   At the end of each month the Incredible
    has credited him with 0.62% interest.   How much has he now?

UNIT 3
COMMUNICATING WITH BASIC

1 Introduction

It is now possible to show how communication with a BASIC program is arranged when it is running. The PRINT statement has already been encountered, and here facilities for printing messages as well as results are introduced. The usefulness of BASIC then takes a great leap forward with a method of providing values to running programs through the use of variables and the INPUT statement.

2 Printing Captions – more about the PRINT statement

In a complicated program, interpretation of a stream of numbers printed by a running program can be very confusing unless explanatory messages are used in the presentation of results. In a PRINT statement messages or 'strings of characters' can be printed simply by enclosing them in quotation marks. BASIC then knows that what is enclosed by quotes is to be printed literally as it appears - hence the term 'literal information' which is sometimes used to describe messages or character strings.

As an example, consider again the sample program of Unit 1

        1Ø PRINT 2+2
        2Ø END

which produced the numerical result 4. The line

        1Ø PRINT "2+2"

will give quite a different result. Try it.

EXERCISE   Try the program

        1Ø PRINT "2+2 = " 2+2
        2Ø END

Normally several expressions to be printed are separated by commas as in the example

        1Ø PRINT 1,2+2,4+5/7,6.13*7.2

but it is not necessary to include the comma before or after
messages in quotation marks. Of course messages are usually in
English, as in the following example which has two PRINT statements.
Note that when this is run, each PRINT statement starts a new line.

```
1Ø PRINT "THIS PROGRAM EVALUATES 2+2"
2Ø PRINT "THE ANSWER IS "2+2
3Ø END
```

EXERCISE   Invent some programs with (polite) messages in them.

3 Dealing with Large Numbers

Some numbers are too large or too small to be printed conveniently
in the normal way, and so an 'exponential format' used by PRINT
statements and by programmers has been devised. The number is
represented by a convenient number multiplied by a power of 10.   For
example

the speed of light is 30 000 000 000 cm/sec
scientists often write this as 3×10^{10} cm/sec
BASIC might write this as 3.0E10 or 3E10, where E means
'exponent'.
Similarly 2.4E - 23 means 2.4×10^{-23} or
0.000 000 000 000 000 000 000 024

The exponential form is

$$n1En2$$

where $n1$ and $n2$ are numbers and E is the letter E. This is interpreted as

$$n1 \times 10^{n2}$$

It will be found that numbers which are too large to fit into 5
spaces will always be rendered by a PRINT statement into this form.

EXERCISE   Try the program

```
1Ø PRINT "A BIG ONE IS " 1ØØØ/.ØØØ1
2Ø PRINT "AND A SMALL ONE " .ØØØ1/1ØØØ
3Ø END
```

A programmer might also wish to write large numbers compactly,
and he can do so by writing his constants in exponential form.

Therefore the number 540 000 could be written in BASIC in several ways, for example

```
540000              as an integer
540000.0            with a decimal point
5.4E5               decimal point and exponent
54E4                integer and exponent
```

4 Inserting Remarks – the REM statement

Documentation or 'writing up' is an important part of the job of programming, and making a program legible is a part of documenting it. Remarks or comments can be put in the written program which are intended to explain the program but which are not part of the printed output when it is run. The REM (for REMark) statement allows this. It is always good style to use them and they are essential in complicated programs.

The REM statement has the form

line number REM *any remark or comment*

and added to the sample program could be

```
10 REM A PROGRAM TO DEMONSTRATE BASIC
20 PRINT "THIS PROGRAM EVALUATES 2+2"
30 PRINT "THE ANSWER IS "  2+2
40 END
```

5 Providing Data to Running Programs – the INPUT statement

If a calculation is to be repeated several times with different numbers, it is inconvenient to spell out the constants each time by rewriting the program. Instead all programming languages allow the actual numbers to be entered when the program is run. In BASIC the INPUT statement does this. The program is written using symbolic variable names, much as in algebra, and an INPUT statement requests their values. Here is an example showing the INPUT statement and how variables are used instead of numbers.

```
10 INPUT A,B
20 PRINT (A+B)/2
30 END
```

At line 10, the program will request values for A and B. This request is indicated by a prompt from the computer; a '?' is printed

when it is ready.   The programmer has commanded the program to RUN
and waits for the '?' to appear.   He then enters numbers A and B,
with a comma between and a 'carriage return' at the end.   The
computer then continues with the program - in this case to calculate
the arithmetic mean (A+B)/2.

Actually the example is in poor style.   The same computation in a
better form is shown with its flowchart in Fig. 3.1.   The features
added to the program demonstrate four points of good style:

 (i)   REM statements are used to explain the purpose of the
        program.
 (ii)   Before INPUT is requested an explanatory message is typed
        at line 30.
(iii)   The values of A and B are confirmed by the program at
        line 60.
 (iv)   The result is printed with an explanation at line 70.

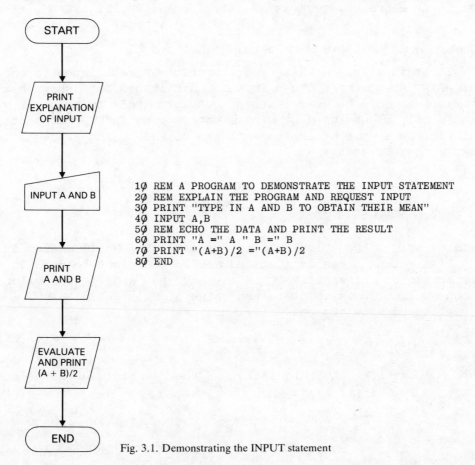

```
1Ø REM A PROGRAM TO DEMONSTRATE THE INPUT STATEMENT
2Ø REM EXPLAIN THE PROGRAM AND REQUEST INPUT
3Ø PRINT "TYPE IN A AND B TO OBTAIN THEIR MEAN"
4Ø INPUT A,B
5Ø REM ECHO THE DATA AND PRINT THE RESULT
6Ø PRINT "A =" A " B =" B
7Ø PRINT "(A+B)/2 ="(A+B)/2
8Ø END
```

Fig. 3.1. Demonstrating the INPUT statement

Exactly two numbers are expected by the INPUT statement at line 40. When the program is run and the '?' appears on the terminal, exactly two numbers should be typed in with a comma between. If the wrong number of values is entered, a self-explanatory message will be issued. They can be in exponential form.

EXERCISE   Run the example, typing different values of A and B. Experiment with different expressions using more and fewer variables. Make deliberate errors in entering values, by entering too many or too few values. Finally, try some numbers in exponential form.

6 BASIC Variables

In the previous section variables A and B were used in an example. There are 286 variable names allowed by BASIC. These are the single letters A to Z and the combination of any single letter followed by any single number, such as AØ, A1, ... A9, BØ, B1 ... B9, etc.*

7 Assignment of Values to Variables – the LET statement

To begin with, in Unit 1, arithmetic was restricted to constants in PRINT statements. Then in this unit it has been shown how variables could be used instead, but up to this point their values could only be assigned by manual entry using INPUT statements. Now it will be seen that assignments can be made using a special statement, the LET statement.

The following is an example

$$2Ø\ LET\ B=3$$

which assigns the value 3 to the variable B. Until statement 20 it is likely that B was not defined and so could not be used in expressions. Alternatively it may have had a different value, but as soon as line 20 is complete the value of B is definitely 3. More complicated ones are possible, such as

$$73\ LET\ D=B\uparrow2-4*A*C$$

which looks like the calculation of the discriminant b^2 - 4ac of the

---

* Note that the letter O (oh) and the number Ø (zero) are easily confused. It is usually obvious what is intended, but when the wrong one has been used in error it can be difficult to spot. A widespread practice, adopted here for the programming examples, is to cross the number Ø (zero).

quadratic equation $ax^2 + bx + c = 0$. A, B and C must be known
before line 73 is reached, otherwise the computer will object.   If
they are known the expression of the right hand side is evaluated
and the result is assigned as the new value of variable D.

The general form of a LET statement is

line number LET *variable = expression*

When a LET statement is encountered, the *expression* on the right
hand side is evaluated. The result replaces the value of the
variable on the left hand side. The effect is therefore in the
assignment of a value to the *variable*.   LET statements are commonly
called assignment statements or replacement statements.

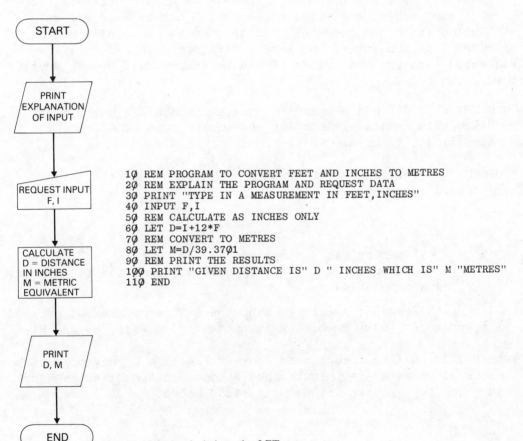

```
1Ø REM PROGRAM TO CONVERT FEET AND INCHES TO METRES
2Ø REM EXPLAIN THE PROGRAM AND REQUEST DATA
3Ø PRINT "TYPE IN A MEASUREMENT IN FEET,INCHES"
4Ø INPUT F,I
5Ø REM CALCULATE AS INCHES ONLY
6Ø LET D=I+12*F
7Ø REM CONVERT TO METRES
8Ø LET M=D/39.37Ø1
9Ø REM PRINT THE RESULTS
1ØØ PRINT "GIVEN DISTANCE IS" D " INCHES WHICH IS" M "METRES"
11Ø END
```

Fig. 3.2. A calculation using LET statements

Example: Suppose a program is converting feet and inches to metres.
The number of inches in a metre is a constant, 39.3701, and so a
constant is used.   The data is requested through an input statement and then converted to inches using a LET statement.   The
value in metres is then calculated with a LET statement, and one
PRINT statement produces the data in inches, along with the metric
equivalent.   The use of LET statements has simplified the PRINT
statement, avoided repetitions of the same calculation which
would be needed to print all the results on one line, and made
the program easy to follow.   The program and flowchart are shown
in Fig. 3.2.

8 Problems

However simple a problem may seem, it is always worthwhile to
prepare a flowchart and write the solution out by hand before
attempting it on the computer.   It is good style to give messages
which explain the nature and layout of input data before it is
requested, and printed output should be accompanied by explanations
too.

PROBLEM 3.1   Write a program to square a number which is typed in.
Using this program search for the square root of 63 to three
significant figures.

PROBLEM 3.2   Write a program which calculates the return r on
compound interest

$$r = (1 + i/100)^n$$

where i = interest rate in per cent
n = number of periods, or number of times the interest has
been compounded.

Using this program, search to find the integer number of periods
n taken to at least double an investment at i = 4%, 6% and 8%.

PROBLEM 3.3   Write a program to convert the time of day on a 24 hour
clock given as hours, minutes and seconds to a decimal time system,
in which for example 18:30:00 is 18.50 hours.

UNIT 4
REPEATING CALCULATIONS

1 Introduction

Many applications of programming in both the business and scientific world require programs to be repeated over and over, perhaps with new data as in processing payroll accounts, or perhaps with some variable changing in a regular way. Several ways of organizing and controlling this kind of repetition will be found in Units which follow, but here the simplest case is introduced and then applied to some quite sophisticated calculations.

2 Repeating Calculations – the GO TO statement

The GO TO statement enables a programmer to change the order in which the statements of a program are obeyed. When a GO TO is encountered, the program jumps to a new place as specified in the GO TO statement. It has the form

line number a GO TO *line number b*

Line number a is just the line number of the statement itself, but *line number b* is another statement of the program which is jumped to. For example

    5Ø GO TO 1Ø

causes the computer to jump to line 10 rather than carrying on to the next line number after 50.

Once a program has been organized to repeat itself, it could go on endlessly unless some way has been organized to stop it. One of the simplest ways is available if the repetition contains an INPUT statement as in Fig. 4.1. In this case, when the program requests data, the programmer can type in STOP.

If a program in a loop is printing continuously, it can be stopped from the terminal. Programming accidents do occur from time to time so every BASIC user should know how to stop a program; the method of doing this varies between systems.

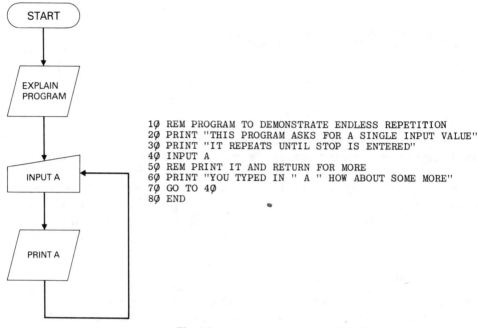

```
1Ø REM PROGRAM TO DEMONSTRATE ENDLESS REPETITION
2Ø PRINT "THIS PROGRAM ASKS FOR A SINGLE INPUT VALUE"
3Ø PRINT "IT REPEATS UNTIL STOP IS ENTERED"
4Ø INPUT A
5Ø REM PRINT IT AND RETURN FOR MORE
6Ø PRINT "YOU TYPED IN " A " HOW ABOUT SOME MORE"
7Ø GO TO 4Ø
8Ø END
```

Fig. 4.1. A program repeated by a GO TO statement

EXERCISE   Find out from an expert how to interrupt a program.   Run and terminate the following example

```
1Ø REM A PAPER EATING PROGRAM
2Ø PRINT "STOP ME"
3Ø GO TO 2Ø
4Ø END
```

3 Self-replacement in LET Statements

It is interesting to enquire what will happen if the same variable is used on both sides in a LET statement, such as

```
99 LET J=J+1
```

The simple answer is that J has been used in calculating its own replacement value. This statement is one of self-replacement and one of its important uses is in counting. A program which counts by ones from 1 is shown in Fig. 4.2, which illustrates an important kind of loop. This is another program requiring manual intervention.

EXERCISE   Try the program of Fig. 4.2.

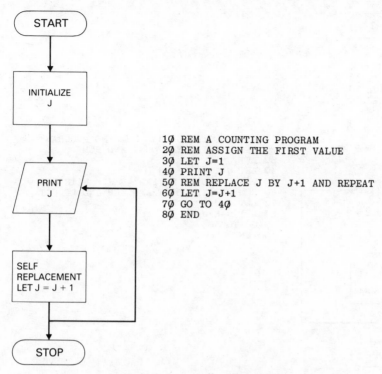

```
1Ø  REM A COUNTING PROGRAM
2Ø  REM ASSIGN THE FIRST VALUE
3Ø  LET J=1
4Ø  PRINT J
5Ø  REM REPLACE J BY J+1 AND REPEAT
6Ø  LET J=J+1
7Ø  GO TO 4Ø
8Ø  END
```

Fig. 4.2. A program to count endlessly

4 Real Programming – recurrence

By looking at self-replacement in more complicated cases than simple counting, it can be seen that a number of useful types of calculation can be undertaken. First of all, it is often useful to be able to add things up. To do this a variable is used to hold the sum which is initialized before the loop, and new additions are made each time around the loop. It is inconvenient at this stage that the loop cannot be stopped automatically, but this disadvantage will be removed in the next Unit.

Fig. 4.3 shows a program that counts from 1 by ones and adds up the total counts at the same time to find 1+2+3... It is similar in structure to Fig. 4.2 but with a sum built in.

EXERCISE   Run the program of Fig. 4.3. Recall that it must be stopped manually. If the formula for the sum of an arithmetic progression is known, check the results.

There is no reason why the self-replacement cannot be of a more

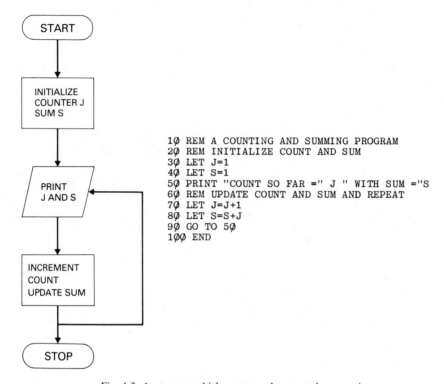

```
10 REM A COUNTING AND SUMMING PROGRAM
20 REM INITIALIZE COUNT AND SUM
30 LET J=1
40 LET S=1
50 PRINT "COUNT SO FAR =" J " WITH SUM ="S
60 REM UPDATE COUNT AND SUM AND REPEAT
70 LET J=J+1
80 LET S=S+J
90 GO TO 50
100 END
```

Fig. 4.3. A program which counts and sums at the same time

complicated type. Here is a program which forms successive squares of a number typed in.

```
10 REM FORM SUCCESSIVE SQUARES OF A NUMBER
20 PRINT "TYPE NUMBER FOR SUCCESSIVE SQUARING"
30 INPUT A
40 PRINT A "SQUARED IS" A*A
50 LET A=A*A
60 GO TO 40
70 END
```

One important use of this kind of loop is called recurrence. This arises when a sum of complicated terms is being found, but the clever programmer can see some relationship between the terms which makes his calculation more efficient. For example suppose the sum is

$$1 + x + x^2 + \ldots$$

A clever programmer would realize that raising a number to a power is expensive in terms of computer time and that each new term is just the previous one multiplied by x. In his program at line 120 the new term is calculated as follows:

```
1Ø REM SUM POWERS OF X
2Ø PRINT "TYPE IN A NUMBER TO SUM ITS POWERS"
3Ø INPUT X
4Ø REM INITIALIZE COUNT J, TERM T, AND SUM S
5Ø LET S=Ø
6Ø LET T=X
7Ø LET J=1
8Ø REM ADD ON LATEST TERM
9Ø LET S=S+T
1ØØ PRINT "TERM" J "IS" T " SUM IS" S
11Ø REM MOVE TO NEXT TERM
12Ø LET J=J+1
13Ø LET T=T*X
14Ø GO TO 9Ø
15Ø END
```

EXERCISE   For x between -1 and 1 the series $1+x+x^2+...$ taken to many terms eventually becomes $1/(1-x)$. Try the program and check the result.

5 Problems

PROBLEM 4.1   Write a program which prints successive powers of 2 in an endless loop. It will have to be stopped manually.

PROBLEM 4.2   Your computer will have a limit to size of numbers it can cope with. Find this limit roughly by successive squaring of 10 (10, 10^2, 10^4, 10^8, etc.) and then try to locate it more accurately. You may be surprised at how large it is.

PROBLEM 4.3   Write a program which adds up numbers you enter at the terminal and counts them as well. Each time round print the count, the sum, and the average so far.

PROBLEM 4.4   The Maclaurin series for e^x is

$$e^x = 1 + x + \frac{x^2}{2} + \frac{x^3}{3!} + \frac{x^4}{4!} + ...$$

Discover a recurrence relationship between terms and write a program to make the sum in an endless loop.

UNIT 5
MAKING DECISIONS

1 Introduction

A powerful and fundamental facility of all computer languages is the ability to compare or test quantities in order to decide the course of the calculation. In other words, a kind of GO TO can be arranged to happen only when certain conditions are satisfied. This is probably the most important single advance to be made in any Unit and it is worth considerable effort. Using the material presented to the end of this Unit, most applications of computing are possible. The Units which follow may introduce facilities of great convenience, but the foundations are laid in the first five Units.

2 Relational Expressions

So far the expressions encountered in BASIC have been those of simple arithmetic, involving the operations +, -, *, /, and ↑. A different kind of expression is the relational expression which is used to make comparisons between quantities or expressions. In BASIC a relational expression decides whether a relationship between two quantities is TRUE or FALSE.

For example the relational expression

$$A > 1\emptyset * B$$

will be TRUE if A is greater than 1∅*B, otherwise it is FALSE. TRUE and FALSE are the only possible results of a relational expression.

The general form of a relational expression is

arithmetic	*relational*	*arithmetic*
expression	*operator*	*expression*

Therefore any two arithmetic expressions can be compared. The available relational operators are

=	equal to	>= or =>	greater or equal
>	greater than	<= or =<	less or equal
<	less than	<> or ><	not equal

Examples:

$$10 > 10 \text{ is FALSE}$$
$$10 = 10 \text{ is TRUE}$$
$$5 <= 6 \text{ is TRUE}$$
A = B   is TRUE if A equals B,
        otherwise FALSE

$B^2 - 4*A*C < 0$ only one
$B^2 - 4*A*C = 0$ of these
                    can be
$B^2 - 4*A*C > 0$ TRUE

3 Decisions – the IF ... THEN statement

The IF...THEN statement uses a relational expression to make a
decision about whether or not to jump to a chosen line number. This
allows programs to determine their own course of events based on
conditions that arise while running. The form of the IF...THEN
statement is

line number a IF *relational expression* THEN *line number b*

Line number a is the line number of the statement itself. When the
computer encounters it, a decision is made about which line to
execute next. If the *relational expression* is TRUE, the computer
jumps to *line number b* as if a GO TO had sent it there. If the
relational expression is FALSE, then the next line in sequence
after *line number a* is executed next in the normal way.

Example:

```
20 IF I=10 THEN 50
30
40
50
```

In this example, when execution reaches line 20, the value of I
is compared to 10. If I=10 then the program jumps to line 50.
Otherwise it continues in the usual way with line 30. Therefore
a way of skipping directly to line 50 has been provided if I=10
at line 20.

Example: The counting program which was presented in Fig. 4.2 can
be made to stop after the fifth term by replacing line 70 with

```
70 IF J<=5 THEN 40
```

which produces the program shown in Fig. 5.1.

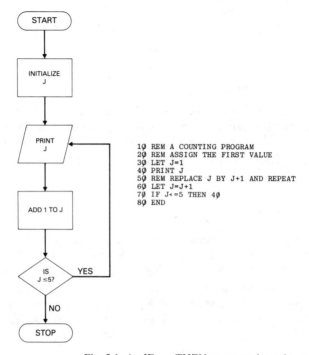

```
10 REM A COUNTING PROGRAM
20 REM ASSIGN THE FIRST VALUE
30 LET J=1
40 PRINT J
50 REM REPLACE J BY J+1 AND REPEAT
60 LET J=J+1
70 IF J<=5 THEN 40
80 END
```

Fig. 5.1. An IF . . . THEN statement is used to stop counting

EXERCISE   Modify the program of Fig. 4.3 to stop after 10 terms have
   been summed and printed.   Draw the modified flowchart.

   In introducing the IF...THEN facility it is necessary to make a
few remarks about program style.   Armed with this decision maker it
is possible to create very involved programs, but it is poor style
to have a more complex structure than is necessary.   Good programs
generally read from the top down without involved jumps back and
forth.   One fault shared by many inexperienced programmers is a tend-
ency to follow an IF...THEN immediately by an unnecessary GO TO.
Looking again at the counting program, Fig. 4.2, the change could
have been to add a line

            65 IF J >5 THEN 80

so that it is followed at line 70 by a GO TO.   This is terrible
style as can be seen by considering how this would complicate the
flowchart of Fig. 5.1.

While standards of documentation may vary considerably, the flow-chart is a universal feature. It should be used by programmers in the design of programs of any complexity, and the finished program should be accompanied by a complete flowchart. Fig. 5.2 shows the meaning of the various flowchart shapes used in this text.

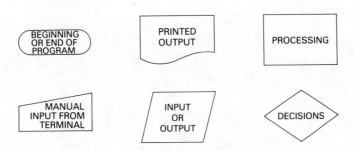

Fig. 5.2. Conventional symbols for flowcharts.

4 A Real Problem – Newton's method

It is now possible to attempt more interesting calculations. Because of the decision making feature these programs will be more complex than before. In this section, the procedures involved in designing and implementing a fairly typical numerical problem are gone over in some detail.

The problem to be considered is the Newton–Raphson method for solving an equation such as

$$f(x) = 0$$

to find values of x which satisfy the equation. The method is based on the simple notion that if a guess is made at the answer, the slope of the function can be used to find a better answer.

In Fig. 5.3 at $x = g$ (for guess) f is the function value and p is the slope. Then a better guess will be at b where it can be shown that

$$b = g - \frac{f}{p}$$

All that is needed is an equation for $f(x)$ and its slope p.

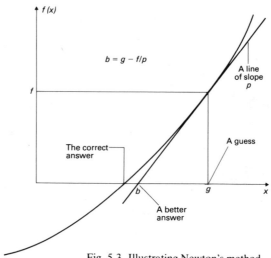

Fig. 5.3. Illustrating Newton's method.

Consider the specific problem now of finding the square root of 2. $f(x)$ becomes

$$x^2 - 2 = 0$$

which has the solution $\sqrt{2}$. The slope of this function is $2x$. Therefore, to find $\sqrt{2}$, a guess g is made, and the slope calculated at g. A better guess b is then calculated from it. The tricky part is then to consider b to be the crude guess and calculate a further improved root, and so on. We use the same statements each time around to give better and better values of b - and this is another example of recurrence.

To implement this method, first a flowchart is drawn to make sure that the procedure is understood. The flowchart for this example is shown in Fig. 5.4. Particular notice should be taken of the replacement of g by b in the return path. This causes each improved estimate to be used again so that further improvements are obtained automatically. As a matter of good practice, it should be noted that the programmer has decided to print the results of every calculation in the procedure. This is always worthwhile because new programs are almost certain to contain mistakes. A liberal spread of PRINT statements throughout a calculation is always useful. To find mistakes in a program it is essential to be able to locate where trouble first appears, and this can only be done with a generous amount of information.

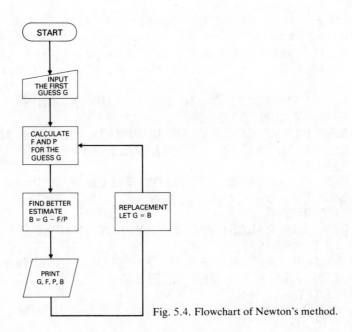

Fig. 5.4. Flowchart of Newton's method.

In order to translate Fig. 5.4 into BASIC, suitable variable names are chosen, in this case

F to represent $f(x)$ G to represent g, the guess

P to represent p, the slope B to represent b, the better guess

By referring to the flowchart, the program can be written out in skeleton form and checked carefully before it is typed into the terminal and tried. The following is a possible solution:

```
1Ø PRINT "TYPE IN A GUESS AT SQR(2)"
2Ø INPUT G
3Ø LET F=G*G-2
4Ø LET P=2*G
5Ø LET B=G-F/P
6Ø PRINT "AT" G "F IS" F "SLOPE" P "NEW GUESS" B
```

```
70 LET G=B
80 GO TO 30
90 END
```

The next stage is to dress the program up with REM statements so that it can be understood if it is looked at by someone else, or indeed by the original programmer after the passage of time. This example is considerably improved by the addition of remarks:

```
10 REM CALCULATION OF SQR(2) BY NEWTON'S METHOD
20 REM BY SOLVING X↑2-2 = 0
30 REM FIRST ACCEPT AN ESTIMATE OF THE ANSWER
40 PRINT "TYPE IN AN ESTIMATE OF SQR(2)"
50 INPUT G
60 REM CALCULATE FUNCTION VALUE F AND SLOPE P
70 LET F=G*G-2
80 LET P=2*G
90 REM NOW CALCULATE AN IMPROVED GUESS B
100 LET B=G-F/P
110 PRINT "AT" G "F IS" F "SLOPE" P "NEW GUESS" B
120 REM USE B AS THE ESTIMATE NEXT TIME ROUND
130 LET G=B
140 GO TO 70
150 END
```

EXERCISE   Try this program. As yet it has no IF...THEN statements.
   Now improve it in two ways. First of all after line 40 check
   that the estimate is between 0 and 2 - otherwise the guess is
   silly. Secondly before line 130 calculate how different B is
   from G, and stop if the difference is less than 0.000 01. The
   square root of 2 is 1.414... Does this program work? Draw a
   flowchart of it.

5 Another Decider – the ON . . . GO TO statement

It is sometimes useful to be able to jump to one of several destinations in a program. The ON...GO TO statement arranges this although it is used much less often than IF...THEN. Its form is

line number ON *expression* GO TO *line number a, line number b,*...

When this statement is reached, the *expression* is worked out. Then if the integer part of the result is 1, the program jumps to *line number a,* if 2 it jumps to *line number b* and so on for however many destinations are given.   If the expression turns out to be negative, zero, or larger than the number of destinations given, then an error has been made and a suitable message will appear on the terminal.

6 Problems

PROBLEM 5.1   Write a program which prints successive powers of 2 and stops after 2^{10}.

PROBLEM 5.2   Rewrite the program for Newton's method to find the square root of any number.   Only accept guesses between 0 and the number whose square root is sought.   Stop the calculation with an IF...THEN statement when the answer ceases to change appreciably.

PROBLEM 5.3   Write a program to find the roots of a quadratic equation $ax^2 + bx + c = 0$ where a, b, and c are given as input from the terminal.   Use an ON...GO TO statement to separate the three possible conditions that will arise in the discriminant. This will require some thought.

PROBLEM 5.4   Write a program to find a root of an equation $ax^3 + bx^2 + cx + d = 0$ where a, b, c, and d are given as input from the terminal using Newton's method.   Ask for help with the expression for slope if necessary.   Find a root of $x^3 - 7.8x + 18.5x - 11.3 = 0$ using this program.   Does it work for any guess?   Draw the function to see why – use BASIC to tabulate values of the function.

UNIT 6
BUILT IN FUNCTIONS

1 Introduction

   Certain calculations tend to occur over and over again in BASIC programs, and many of these use the values of common functions which are not easy to compute. The calculation of a square root is a good example of this; it is obviously not desirable to have to write out a program such as in Unit 5 to calculate the square root every time one is needed. Like all computer languages, BASIC has built in 'library' functions which evaluate often-used functions. To find a square root the SQR function is used.

2 Library Functions in BASIC

   The list of functions available in BASIC varies considerably between systems. All versions include the following mathematical ones:

FUNCTION	MEANING
SQR(*expression*)	Square root of *expression*
ABS(*expression*)	Absolute value of *expression*
SGN(*expression*)	Sign of *expression*, 1 if >0, 0 if 0, −1 if <0
INT(*expression*)	Largest integer not greater than *expression*
EXP(*expression*)	The value of $e^{expression}$
LOG(*expression*)	Natural logarithm (base e) of *expression*
SIN(*expression*)	Sine of *expression*, *expression* in radians
COS(*expression*)	Cosine of *expression*, *expression* in radians
TAN(*expression*)	Tangent of *expression*, *expression* in radians
ATN(*expression*)	The angle in the range $-\pi/2$ to $\pi/2$ radians whose tangent is *expression*

A function RND which is a random number generator also appears in most versions of BASIC.

To use a function, simply write it into any expression where it is

desired with its 'argument' in brackets immediately after it.   For
example:

        2Ø PRINT SQR(2)

prints the square root of 2.

3 Trying Them Out

Here the functions given in the previous section are considered
individually, except for INT which is looked at in detail later.

(a) SQR

The square root function saves a programmer the trouble of
devising a numerical method for finding square roots every time he
needs one.   The only thing to remember when using it is that a
negative number does not have a real square root.   The following
program uses SQR to find the hypoteneuse of a right-angled triangle,
given the other two sides:

        1Ø PRINT "THIS PROGRAM FINDS THE HYPOTENEUSE"
        2Ø PRINT "TYPE IN TWO SIDES"
        3Ø INPUT A,B
        4Ø PRINT "HYPOTENEUSE=" SQR(A*A+B*B)
        5Ø GO TO 2Ø
        6Ø END

EXERCISE   Try this example.   It will give no trouble about negative
    arguments.   Then find out what happens if SQR is given a negative
    argument.

(b) ABS

This function forces the sign of an expression to be positive.
It can be used to keep out of trouble with SQR, as in

        6ØØ LET T=SQR(ABS(X))

Very often a program is interested in the size of a value regardless
of its sign, and this is when ABS is used.   In some problems in
Unit 7 the size of a term in a power series will be used to stop
adding more terms.

(c) SGN

Sometimes it may be important to know when a number is positive
or negative independently of the value.   Problem 5.3 was difficult

without the SGN function. To test the discriminant of a quadratic expression $Ax^2 + Bx + C$ an ON...GO TO statement can be used with

$$SGN(B*B-4*A*C)+2$$

which has the values 1, 2, or 3 for negative, zero or positive values of the discriminant.

   It can be used to transfer the sign of one variable to another. Suppose Z is to have the same magnitude as X but the same sign as Y. This can be achieved by combining the SGN and ABS functions as in

$$90 \text{ LET } Z=SGN(Y)*ABS(X)$$

which will work except when Y is zero.

(d) EXP and LOG

   These two mathematical functions go together, and are based on e or 2.718 281 828 45 the base of natural logarithms. The EXP function provides e raised to a power, and LOG finds the logarithm to the base e. Therefore if

$$Y = EXP(X) \quad \text{then} \quad X = LOG(Y)$$

The log function can easily be used to base 10 or any other base by recalling that

$$\log_a X = \log_e X \, \log_a e = \frac{\log_e X}{\log_e a}$$

so that the log of X to base 10 could be found using a statement like

$$110 \text{ LET } L=LOG(X)/LOG(10)$$

or to base A by

$$110 \text{ LET } L=LOG(X)/LOG(A)$$

EXERCISE   Print the value of e.

(e) SIN, COS, and TAN

   These trigonometric functions of an angle as illustrated in Fig. 6.1, are often used. In BASIC the angle is in radians and this may not always be convenient, although conversion is easy since π radians is the same as 180°. A simple way to calculate π is mentioned under the ATN function which follows.

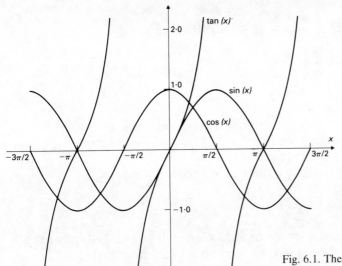

Fig. 6.1. The trigonometric functions.

EXERCISE   Check using the BASIC functions for a few angles that
(i) $\sin^2 x + \cos^2 x = 1$,   (ii) $\tan x = \sin x / \cos x$

(f) ATN

The ATN or arc tangent function is one which can give conceptual
difficulty. The argument of the function is the value of a tangent,
and the result is the angle that goes with it. For example the
tangent of 45° is 1. Therefore the function

ATN(1)

gives the angle in radians whose tangent is 1, i.e., $\pi/4$ radians.
This useful result can be used to convert degrees to radians and
vice versa.

Often the value of π is wanted. This can be derived by writing

100 LET P=4*ATN(1)

There is an ambiguity in the ATN function because if the tangent
is x, then the angle could be A, say, but also $A \pm \pi/2$, $A \pm \pi$, and
so on. This is why the ATN function gives an answer between $-\pi/2$
and $\pi/2$, which is an unambiguous range as can be seen in Fig. 6.1.

4 Truncation and Its Uses

Probably the most useful function of them all is the INT function.
Because of its importance it is discussed here separately. Precisely
speaking, INT(x) provides a value which is the largest integer which
is not greater than x. Accordingly

INT(5.95) is 5   and   INT(-5.95) is -6

Look carefully at the second example.

(a)   Rounding

Often it is necessary to round a result to the nearest whole number, or to a certain number of decimal places.   Although INT does not do this directly, it is easily forced to do so.   To round x to the nearest whole number, simply add 0.5 before using INT:

        4ØØ LET Y=INT(X+0.5)

A simple extension to this idea enables rounding to be taken to any scale.   Scale the data so that the resolution desired is represented by successive integers, add 0.5, and then reverse the scaling.

Examples:

    (i) Round to two decimal places (to the nearest 0.01)

        4ØØ LET Y=INT(X*1ØØ+Ø.5)/1ØØ

    (ii) Round to the nearest 100

        4ØØ LET Y=INT(X/1ØØ+Ø.5)*1ØØ

    (iii) Round to nearest 4

        4ØØ LET Y=INT(X/4+Ø.5)*4

(b)   Truncation

The term truncation applies to the removal of decimal places, and so the function INT as it stands is not quite a truncation because of its operation on negative numbers.   However an expression

        SGN(X)*INT(ABS(X))

does truncate as does INT itself for positive numbers.

Truncation is useful when the remainder after division is required.   This happens when numbers are being converted from one base to another and when units are being converted.   In dividing 22 by 7 the integer part of the quotient is 3 and the remainder is 1. If the quotient were N/D with N positive, then the integer part would be

$$INT(N/D)$$

and the remainder

$$N-INT(N/D)*D$$

However if N or D could be negative, the integer part would be

$$SGN(N/D)*INT(ABS(N/D))$$

and the unsigned remainder is

$$ABS(N)-INT(ABS(N/D))*ABS(D)$$

(c)   Base conversion

To convert numbers between bases, the old number is divided by the new base over and over again with the remainders forming the number in the new base.

Example: 131 decimal to base 7

Step 1	131/7 =	18 remainder	5
Step 2	18/7 =	2 remainder	4
Step 3	2/7 =	0 remainder	2

The answer is 5 units, 4 sevens, and 2 forty-nines, i.e., 245 in base 7.

(d)   Units conversion

There are many cases of units of measurement with mixed bases, particularly in the English system. For example a time measurement in days, hours, minutes and seconds is in bases 24, 60 and 60. To convert 18.43 days into hours, minutes and seconds requires the following BASIC statements:

```
100 REM GET WHOLE HOURS
110 LET H=INT(24*18.43)
120 REM REMAINING PART HOUR
130 LET R=18.43*24-H
140 REM WHOLE MINUTES
150 LET M=INT(60*R)
160 REM REMAINING PART MINUTE
170 LET R=60*R-M
180 REM FINALLY SECONDS WITH DECIMAL PLACES
190 LET S=60*R
```

At the end the time is in variables H, M and S.

5 Problems

PROBLEM 6.1   The period T seconds of a pendulum of length ℓ metres
for a small angle of swing is

$$T = 2\pi\sqrt{\ell/g}$$

where g = 9.81 metres/sec^2.

(a)   Write a program to find the period from the length.
(b)   Write a program to find the length from the period.
Check these programs against each other.

PROBLEM 6.2   Given the two sides adjacent to the right angle in a
triangle, calculate the length of the hypoteneuse and find the
other two angles in degrees.

PROBLEM 6.3   Write a program to convert a decimal number to any
base from 2 to 9.   Do this in a loop;   it is acceptable that the
results are produced in reverse order.   Make it work for positive
or negative numbers.

UNIT 7
PROGRAM LOOPS

1 Introduction

In many earlier problems and examples, programs were encountered which included repeated calculations or loops. It has been seen how an IF...THEN statement is used to control a loop. In many calculations the number of repetitions of a loop is predetermined and in these cases BASIC has a special facility for organizing them.

2 Forming Loop

Many programs require calculations to be repeated a fixed number of times. Loops can be set up and controlled using a LET statement for initialization and counting, and an IF...THEN statement to test for completion. Initialization, counting, and testing are the common features of a counting loop.

Suppose a calculation is to be repeated 10 times. A variable I can be set aside to count the number of times the loop has been executed. Before a loop is entered, I is initialized by being set to one. Each time the end of the loop is reached, I is increased by one and then tested to see if the loop is complete. Figure 7.1 illustrates a typical flowchart for looping.

3 The Easy Way – the FOR and NEXT statements

BASIC has two special statements to make loop formation easier for a programmer. The definition of the loop is accomplished by a FOR statement which gives all the information about the initial and final values of the counter and the step size in between. The NEXT statement identifies the end of the loop.

As an example, suppose a variable I is to be used to count 10 passes around a loop. Then the FOR and NEXT statements could be as follows:

```
7Ø  FOR  I=1  TO  1Ø
8Ø
9Ø
1ØØ  (A CALCULATION)
11Ø
12Ø
13Ø  NEXT  I
```

The convenience of this is obvious. The general form of the FOR statement is

line number FOR *variable* = *expression* TO *expression* STEP *expression*

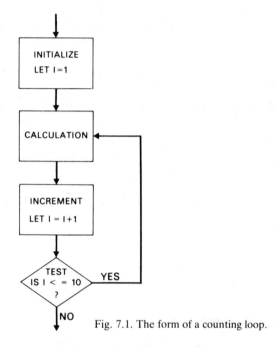

Fig. 7.1. The form of a counting loop.

The meaning of the statement should be quite clear although there are a number of rules of detail which the following points should clarify:

    (i) A variable name must be used as the index or loop counter. It does not have to be referred to in the calculation itself, as in this example using K as a counter

```
1Ø  FOR  K=1  TO  5
2Ø  PRINT  "LOOP"
3Ø  NEXT  K
```

(ii)   The initial and final values are given in the FOR statement.

(iii) The STEP part is optional. If STEP is left out, the step
       size is 1. It can be fractional or negative as in

   1Ø FOR X=.25 TO 1.5Ø STEP .25
        .
        .
        .
   8Ø NEXT X

   and

   2ØØ FOR P=1Ø TO 1 STEP -1
        .
        .
        .
   53Ø NEXT P

(iv)   The limits and the step size can be any expression.

 (v)   If the initial, final, and step values are such that the
       loop should not be executed, it is jumped over. Thus the
       loop

   66 FOR J=1Ø TO 1 STEP 2
        .
        .
        .
   99 NEXT J

   is skipped over without any of it being executed.

(vi)   The initial, final, and step values are considered only
       when the loop is entered the first time so that they
       cannot later be altered. For example

   5Ø FOR I=J TO K STEP L
   6Ø LET L=L*2
   7Ø LET K=K-1
   8Ø NEXT I

   If J, K, and L are 1, 10, and 1 the loop is repeated 10
   times. The changes made to K and L inside the loop do
   not alter this.

(vii) The value of the loop variable itself can be changed
       inside the loop and this *will* affect its operation. For
       example

   5Ø FOR I=1 TO 1Ø
   6Ø LET I=I+1
   7Ø NEXT I

is only repeated 5 times. Be sure that the difference between this and rule (vi) is understood.

(viii) Computers can make slight errors when dealing with non-integers, and fail to hit an exact final value which could mean the loop will be executed an extra time. For example

```
10 LET T=ATN(1)
20 LET S=T/7
30 FOR I=S TO T STEP S
40 NEXT I
```

might be executed 8 rather than 7 times because the 7th time S is added to I, it might fall fractionally short of T.

(ix) Loops can be abandoned; an IF...THEN or a GO TO within the loop could make the program leave it entirely.

(x) Loops can be jumped into from outside if care is taken to give the index a suitable value. Jumping out and then back in can be useful although this is usually unnecessary and is considered poor style.

To match every FOR statement there must be a NEXT statement. The NEXT statement takes the form

line number NEXT *variable*

which indicates the end of the loop. The named variable is the same loop index as appeared in the FOR statement.

Example: The factorial of an integer is the product of all integers up to and including the number. The factorial of 0 is 1. Here is a program segment to evaluate the factorial of N which works for 0 and any positive integer

```
80 REM EVALUATE FACTORIAL N
90 REM INITIALIZE FACTORIAL
100 LET F=1
110 REM FORM PRODUCT OF ALL INTEGERS TO N
120 FOR K=N TO 1 STEP -1
130 LET F=F*K
140 NEXT K
150 PRINT "FACTORIAL IS" F
```

4 Nesting FOR and NEXT Loops

Programs will often require several loops contained within one another. This is allowed by BASIC as long as they do not overlap because if they did the intention of the program would be ambiguous. If they are correctly arranged they are said to be nested. Two examples serve to illustrate correct and incorrect arrangements.

<table>
<tr><td>Correct</td><td>Incorrect</td></tr>
<tr><td>The loops are 'nested'</td><td>The loops cross</td></tr>
</table>

Correct	Incorrect
1Ø FOR I=1 TO 1Ø	1Ø FOR I=1 TO 1Ø
. . .	. . .
3Ø FOR J=1 TO 5	3Ø FOR J=1 TO 5
. . .	. . .
5Ø NEXT J	5Ø NEXT I
. . .	. . .
7Ø NEXT I	7Ø NEXT J

The same variable cannot be used as counter in nested loops, as follows:

```
1Ø  FOR  I=1  TO  1Ø
3Ø  FOR  I=1  TO  5       not allowed
5Ø  NEXT  I
7Ø  NEXT  I
```

Example: Here is a program which prints a table of compound interest return on 100 units invested at 6%, 7%, 8% and 9% for up to 10 compoundings. The return r on principal p invested at i% for n period is

$$r = p(1 + i/100)^n$$

which is evaluated in nested loops for *i* from 6 to 9 and for *n* from 1 to 10. The print feature used gives a taste of things to come in the next unit.

```
1ØØ  REM PROGRAM TO PRINT INVESTMENT TABLE
11Ø  PRINT"            TABLE  OF  RETURN  ON  INVESTMENT"
12Ø  PRINT
13Ø  PRINT "RATE",6,7,8,9
14Ø  REM REPEAT ON NEW LINE FOR 1 TO 1Ø PERIODS
15Ø  FOR N=1 TO 1Ø
```

```
16Ø PRINT "PERIOD" N,
17Ø REM PRINT ON ONE LINE FOR RATES 6 TO 9
18Ø FOR I=6 TO 9
19Ø PRINT 1ØØ*(1+I/1ØØ)↑N,
2ØØ NEXT I
21Ø NEXT N
22Ø END
```

5 Problems

There are more problems here than earlier; the last few are quite difficult.

PROBLEM 7.1   The Maclaurin series for sin x is

$$\sin x = x - \frac{x^3}{3!} + \frac{x^5}{5!} - \frac{x^7}{7!} + \ldots$$

Write a program to evaluate 10 terms of this and compare it with the built-in SIN function for various values of x.

PROBLEM 7.2   Now improve on the solution to 7.1.   Be sure an efficient recurrence is being used.   Before evaluating the series scale x into the range $-\pi$ to π using a remainder.   Limit the loop to however many repetitions are certain to produce a result correct to 5 figures for any value of x but jump out of the loop earlier if the error indicated by the most recent term is small enough.

PROBLEM 7.3   An example in this Unit shows how to calculate a factorial N!   The formulae for permutations and combinations are

$_n P_r$ = number of arrangements (permutations) of n things taken r at a time

$$= \frac{n!}{(n-r)!}$$

$_n C_r$ = number of combinations of n things taken r at a time

$$= \frac{n!}{r!(n-r)!}$$

Write programs to calculate nCr and nPr where n and r are typed in.   Use factorials.

PROBLEM 7.4   Calculate and print nCr over the range $n = 0, 1, \ldots,$ 10 and $r = 0, 1, \ldots, n$.   Copy the PRINT arrangement from the investment table example to make all the results for a given n appear on the same line.

PROBLEM 7.5   A prime number is one which has no factors other than itself or unity.   33 is not a prime number since it can be resolved into factors 3 and 11.   3 and 11 are prime numbers. Write a program to determine whether a number typed in is prime. To find out if a number i is prime, test for a zero remainder after division by every integer from 2 to $\sqrt{i}$ - if any is found i is not prime.

PROBLEM 7.6   Write a program to find and print all the primes less than 100.

PROBLEM 7.7   Write a program to find all the prime factors of a number which is typed in.

PROBLEM 7.8   One method of finding the area under a curve is the trapezoidal rule;   see Fig. 7.2.

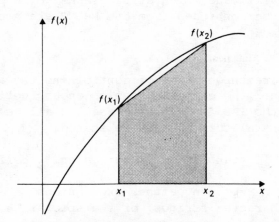

Fig. 7.2. Illustrating the trapezoidal rule.

The area a of the shaded trapezoid is
$$a = \frac{f(x_1) + f(x_2)}{2} (x_2 - x_1)$$

By dividing the range $0 < x < 1$ into N trapezoids, find the area under the curve $e^{-x^2/2}$ from $x = 0$ to $x = 1$. N is to be typed in. How big must N be for 0.1% accuracy?

UNIT 8
PRINTING AND GRAPH PLOTTING

1 Introduction

The PRINT statement provides several ways of controlling the layout of printed lines. Some of these facilities have been demonstrated
already, and the remaining features are described here. In simple
BASIC the placement and spacing of numerical output can be controlled
only to a limited extent. However in a different way BASIC is highly
versatile in the facilities which allow graphs to be plotted and
lines of output to be continued from one PRINT statement to the next.

2 Another Look at the PRINT Statement

In BASIC there are three means of controlling the alignment of
printed information: the comma and semicolon as 'delimiters' and a
special function, the TAB function. These are all used in the PRINT
statement whose general form can now be stated:

line number PRINT *quantity delimiter quantity delimiter*

where   *quantity* can represent either expressions of any complexity,
               character strings, or the special TAB function
        delimiter can be a comma or a semicolon, and sometimes can be
               omitted.

Example:
        75 PRINT A,B+C,TAB(D); "CHARACTER STRING"

Quantities: A   Delimiters: , (comma)
              B+C   ; (semicolon)
              TAB(D)
              "CHARACTER STRING"

3 Printing with Commas

Whenever quantities to be printed are separated by commas, BASIC
divides the output line into 5 zones of 15 spaces each. Numbers are
always printed in the same five zones regardless of their size or
type of presentation. In this way BASIC can print tables containing

five or fewer columns, which will always be aligned.

EXERCISE   Investigate the printing of numbers by BASIC:

     (i) Look at how integers are presented. Find out how large they
          are before they are printed in exponential format.
    (ii) Look at non-integers and their printing in exponential format.
 (iii) Find out what happens if more than five numbers are printed.

    The printing of character strings is similar, but if the message
is longer than 15 characters there will be a skip to the next occupied
zone.

    One new feature of printing with commas is the ability of BASIC
to continue new statements on the same line, as in

```
60 FOR I=1 TO 5
70 PRINT I,
80 NEXT I
90 END
```

which will print the five values of I on the same line. To force a
new line, use another PRINT statement, as in

```
10 FOR I=1 TO 5
20 FOR J=1 TO 5
30 PRINT I,
40 NEXT J
50 PRINT
60 NEXT I
70 END
```

EXERCISE   Try this new feature.

4 Printing with Semicolons

    If a semicolon is used in place of a comma in PRINT statements,
then the printed output is squeezed together. The result is that
more numbers can be printed on a line. Unfortunately the size of
the zones varies according to the number of digits in the result.
For small integers the zone is 6 places.

    Another use of the semicolon is in continuing printed output on
the same line with several PRINT statements. If a semicolon is used
as delimiter after the last quantity in a PRINT statement, then the
next PRINT statement to be obeyed will continue on the same line as
in

```
1Ø  FOR  I=1. TO  1Ø
2Ø  PRINT  I;
3Ø  NEXT  I
4Ø  END
```

A PRINT statement with no quantities or delimiters will cause a new
line, as would any PRINT statement without a final delimiter:

```
1Ø  FOR  I=1  TO  5
2Ø  PRINT  I;
3Ø  FOR  J=1  TO  5
4Ø  PRINT  J;
5Ø  NEXT  J
6Ø  PRINT
7Ø  NEXT  I
8Ø  END
```

This same feature is useful when asking for input from a terminal.
A message can be given with a PRINT statement ending with a semicolon. The prompt and response to the INPUT statement can then follow
on the same line. This makes a convenient and neat dialogue as in

```
3Ø  PRINT  "WHAT  IS  N";
4Ø  INPUT  N
```

EXERCISE   Try these features.

5 Printer Zoning – the TAB function

When the special TAB function and the semicolon are used together
a large measure of control over printer zoning and graph plotting is
available. TAB is a special function which can only be used in PRINT
statements. It appears with a single argument such as TAB(x), where
x could be an expression of any complexity. It causes the printer to
move along the printed line to the column given by the integer part
of x, which should be an existing column number. Thus x should not
be either negative or too large for the printer. TAB(x) is normally
followed by a semicolon so that printing will begin in the next
space, i.e. at column INT(x) + 1. If TAB(x) were followed by a comma,
then the printer would move to the beginning of the next 15 column
field which is usually wrong.

TAB can therefore place a number or a message exactly where it is
wanted.

EXERCISE   Try the following example:

```
1∅ FOR I=1 TO 1∅
2∅ PRINT TAB(I);  I
3∅ NEXT I
4∅ END
```

It is important to know that the TAB function cannot move the printer backwards, and if it is attempted it will have no effect. To move to column 60 from column 50, TAB(6∅) is used (not TAB(1∅)).

6 An Example – printing Pascal's triangle

Pascal's triangle is the arrangement of the coefficients of binomial expansions in triangular form shown in Fig. 8.1

$$
\begin{array}{ccccccc}
 & & & {}_0C_0 & & & \\
 & & {}_1C_0 & & {}_1C_1 & & \\
 & {}_2C_0 & & {}_2C_1 & & {}_2C_2 & \\
{}_3C_0 & & {}_3C_1 & & {}_3C_2 & & {}_3C_3 \\
{}_4C_0 & {}_4C_1 & {}_4C_2 & {}_4C_3 & {}_4C_4 & & \\
{}_5C_0 & {}_5C_1 & {}_5C_2 & {}_5C_3 & {}_5C_4 & {}_5C_5 & \\
{}_6C_0 & {}_6C_1 & {}_6C_2 & {}_6C_3 & {}_6C_4 & {}_6C_5 & {}_6C_6
\end{array}
$$

Fig. 8.1. Pascal's Triangle.

The quantity nCr was defined in Problem 7.3

$$
{}_nC_r = \frac{n!}{r!\,n-r!}
$$

from which in the search for efficiency, a recurrence can be found

$$
{}_nC_r = \frac{n - r + 1}{r}\,{}_nC_{r-1}
$$

which makes it unnecessary to find any factorials! To print the first line, send the printer to column 35, say, and then move each new line back three spaces so that if each number uses 6 spaces the output will be nicely lined up. Therefore line n begins at column $35-3n$ and the number nCr is in column $35 - 3n + 6r$. The complete program to print 10 lines of Pascal's triangle is:

```
100 REM A PROGRAM TO PRINT PASCAL'S TRIANGLE
110 REM N IS LINE NUMBER
120 FOR N=0 TO 9
130 REM PRINT THE FIRST VALUE ON EACH LINE
140 LET C=1
150 PRINT TAB(35-3*N);C;
160 REM NOW THE REMAINDER OF LINE N
170 FOR R=1 TO N
180 LET C=C*(N-R+1)/R
190 PRINT TAB(35-3*N+6*R);C;
200 NEXT R
210 REM MOVE TO A NEW LINE
220 PRINT
230 NEXT N
240 END
```

EXERCISE   Run this program.

7 Plotting Line Graphs

In printer zoning, character strings can be treated like any other
quantity. Therefore the TAB function can be used to move the printer
to a desired column where a character string can begin. This enables
graphs to be plotted; the printer is advanced to the correct place
and a symbol is printed. To make the graph fit the number of spaces
available usually requires some scaling.

As an example a straight line can be plotted easily by printing in
column one of the first line, column two of the second, and so on.
The program could be

```
10 FOR I=1 TO 10
20 PRINT TAB(I);"*"
30 NEXT I
40 END
```

By representing the curve by one symbol a line graph is produced.
As a more complicated example, a cosine wave is printed of amplitude
25 print positions and period 20 lines. If I is the line number from
0 to 19, then the function is

$$25 \cos \left\{ \frac{2\pi I}{20} \right\}$$

but must be displaced to prevent it from going off the page to the
left. The constant $2\pi/20$ is calculated in advance using the ATN
function. Here is the program; note that the column number is
'rounded' by the addition of 0.5.

```
1Ø LET T=8*ATN(1)/2Ø
2Ø FOR I=Ø TO 19
3Ø PRINT TAB(25.5+25*COS(T*I));"*"
4Ø NEXT
5Ø END
```

EXERCISE   Try these programs.

8 Plotting Bar Graphs

A bar graph has a shaded or solid line drawn in each position.
In BASIC a program calculates where to begin and how many symbols
make up the line before producing it in a FOR...NEXT loop.   An
example of a shaded straight line beginning in column 30 is:

```
1Ø FOR I=1 TO 1Ø
2Ø PRINT TAB(3Ø);
3Ø FOR J=1 TO I
4Ø PRINT "*";
5Ø NEXT J
6Ø PRINT
7Ø NEXT I
8Ø END
```

One special feature which applies to the zoning of character
strings is that the delimiter can be omitted before or after a string
except at the end of a line.   If this is done a semicolon is assumed
except at the end of a line, where printing continued on the same
line must be specified explicitly by a semicolon.

EXERCISE   Run the examples of Sections 6 and 7 of this Unit again,
   omitting unnecessary semicolons.

9 Problems

PROBLEM 8.1   Plot a full cycle of a sine wave on the terminal of
   amplitude 30 print positions and period 30 lines.

PROBLEM 8.2   To a suitable scale plot the polynomial

$$f(x) = x^3 - 7.8x^2 + 18.5x - 11.3$$

PROBLEM 8.3   Plot a full cycle of a cosine wave on the terminal
   with the x-axis shown.

PROBLEM 8.4   Plot a full cycle of a cosine wave and a sine wave
   together with the x-axis shown.

UNIT 9
DEFINING FUNCTIONS

1 Introduction

The standard built-in functions of BASIC have already been introduced. These cover the most common and important requirements for functions. In addition to these it is possible for a program to define its own functions in a restricted but useful way. Functions can shorten or simplify programs by replacing similar expressions which occur frequently in a program.

2 Defining Functions – the DEF FN statement

Anywhere in a BASIC program a one-line function definition can be inserted by the DEF FN statement:

line number DEF FN*a* (*variable*) = *expression*

The function name is FN*a*, where *a* can be any letter of the alphabet, so that the 26 available names are FNA, FNB, ..., FNZ. A given name can only be defined once but can be referred to as often as is desired.

The *variable* in brackets is the argument of the function, and is called a 'dummy argument' because the variable name used in the DEF FN*a* statement is not the variable whose value is used when the function is referred to. The argument will normally appear in the right hand side *expression* but need not. When the function is used by a running program, the expression on the right hand side is evaluated with the value of the argument referred to substituted for the variable in the function definition.

This may sound quite complicated but is really simple and will be illustrated by several examples.

Example: The area of a circle is πr^2, where r is the radius. A function can be defined to find the area of any circle by a statement like

$$3\emptyset \ \text{DEF} \ \text{FNC(R)=4*ATN(1)*R*R}$$

which calculates the area of a circle given its radius as
argument.   Elsewhere in the same BASIC program this could be used,
for example

> 45 PRINT "RADIUS"X"AREA"FNC(X)

so that a complete program to print the areas of circles of
radius 1.0, 1.1, ..., 1.9, could be

```
1Ø REM PROGRAM TO FIND AREAS OF CIRCLES
2Ø REM DEFINE AREA FUNCTION
3Ø DEF FNC(R)=4*ATN(1)*R*R
4Ø REM NOW WORK OUT AREAS
5Ø FOR X=1.Ø TO 1.9 STEP Ø.1
6Ø PRINT"RADIUS "X" AREA "FNC(X)
7Ø NEXT X
8Ø END
```

It should be clear how the function is defined using a dummy
variable R and later referred to using an actual argument X.

Although a function must have an argument, it need not actually
be used.   Functions can refer to other functions but obviously a
function cannot refer to itself, nor can an endless loop of functions
be permitted.

Example: The evaluation of π could be made a function FNP:

> 25 DEF FNP(Z)=4*ATN(1)

in which case the previous function definition could itself use
the defined function FNP

> 3Ø DEF FNR=FNP(Z)*R*R

in which any convenient variable name is used as an argument – it
must have one even though it is not used.

Example: The function FNT provides a true truncation of its
argument

> 6Ø DEF FNT(X)=SGN(X)*INT(ABS(X))

Example: The function FNR rounds its argument to the nearest
integer

> 7Ø DEF FNR(X)=INT(X+Ø.5)

In a function, variables may be used which are not arguments of the function.   If this is done, the real value of the variable is used.   To illustrate this, consider rounding to a particular accuracy as was illustrated in Unit 6.

Example: The function FND rounds its argument X after scaling by a scale factor S, so that S defines the precision of the scaling. After rounding X is restored to its original size but is now rounded to the nearest S.

$$4\emptyset \ \ DEF \ \ FND(X)=(INT(X)/S+\emptyset.5)*S$$

so that with S = 100 rounding is to the nearest 100; with S = 0.01 rounding is to two decimal places.

3 Problems

PROBLEM 9.1   Define functions for hyperbolic sine, cosine, and tangent and plot them over the range $-2 < x < 2$.

$$\sinh x = \frac{e^x - e^{-x}}{2} \qquad\qquad \cosh x = \frac{\sinh x}{\cosh x}$$

$$\tanh x = \frac{\sinh x}{\cosh x}$$

PROBLEM 9.2   Define a function for arc sine using a suitable range of angles.

PROBLEM 9.3   Define a function for arc cosine using a suitable range of angles.

PROBLEM 9.4   Define a function to transfer the sign of a variable S to the function argument.   Try to make it work for S = 0.

PROBLEM 9.5   Define a function to find the remainder when N, the function argument, is divided by D.   Use this to convert

33	to base 7	7600	to base 6
32 767	to base 5	5100	to base 8

UNIT 10
WORKING WITH LISTS

1 Introduction

Most computing languages provide what is called an array facility;
a means of organizing a list of values under only one variable name.
A program can refer to any member of the list by the use of a subscript, and by varying the value of the subscript a common calculation
can be applied throughout the list.

2 Lists and Subscripts

In BASIC an ordered set of values can be given one variable name
and treated as a list. A particular member of the list can be
selected by the use of a subscript. BASIC automatically recognizes
a variable as a list if it is used with a subscript and the subscript
itself can be any expression.

Examples:

$A(3)$ refers to the third entry in the list called A
$B(I+J)$ refers to the $(I+J)$th entry in the list called B

A subscript can be any expression, but it is obvious that it has
to be interpreted as a positive integer. In BASIC the lowest subscript is 1. If the value of the subscript is not an integer, it is
truncated to an integer (truncation or removal of decimal places was
discussed in Unit 6).

Example:

$C(3.75)$ refers to the third entry in the list called C

BASIC checks every subscript as it is used and if subscripts occur
which are less than one or too large the program will not be allowed
to continue. The same variable name should not be used in both subscripted and unsubscripted form in a program. Unsubscripted variables
of the kind used in earlier units are properly called scalar
variables.

The use of lists in programs is demonstrated by a series of examples.

Example: Defining and printing a list

A convenient way of assigning values to a list in advance is described in Unit 12. In the meantime less convenient ways are used. Suppose in a prison with 4 cells, each prisoner has been given a prisoner number. The set of prisoner numbers could form a list in which subscripts correspond to the numbering of the cells, as illustrated by Fig. 10.1.

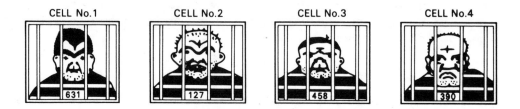

Fig. 10.1. A list of prisoners.

The list is described as

	subscript		value
The prisoner in cell	1	is	631
The prisoner in cell	2	is	127
The prisoner in cell	3	is	458
The prisoner in cell	4	is	390

In a BASIC program, the list of prisoner numbers could be called N. Subscripts 1 to 4 select different cells, and the prisoner numbers are N(1), N(2), N(3) and N(4). The following program reads in the prisoner numbers one at a time and prints them out again. In a FOR...NEXT loop the INPUT statement at line 30 refers to the cell numbers one at a time with subscript I. At line 60 the subscripted variable N(J) prints them as J varies.

```
10 PRINT "TYPE IN THE PRISONER NUMBERS ONE AT A 'TIME"
20 FOR I=1 TO 4
30 INPUT N(I)
40 NEXT I
50 FOR J=4 TO 1 STEP -1
60 PRINT "THE PRISONER IN CELL" J " IS NUMBER" N(J)
70 NEXT J
80 END
```

EXERCISE   Try this program.

Example: Suppose now a search is to be made for the highest prisoner
   number.   To do this a scalar variable H is set aside and given a
   lower initial value than any prisoner number can ever be.   H is
   compared with each prisoner number in turn.   Whenever a higher
   number than H is found, this value replaces H.   At the end H will
   hold the highest number.   This is added on to the previous example:

```
8Ø REM NOW SEARCH FOR THE HIGHEST NUMBER
9Ø LET H=Ø
1ØØ FOR I=1 TO 4
11Ø IF H>=N(I) THEN 13Ø
12Ø LET H=N(I)
13Ø NEXT I
14Ø PRINT "THE HIGHEST NUMBER IS" H
15Ø END
```

EXERCISE   Draw a flowchart for this program and find the deliberate
   error.   Correct it and try the program.   Modify it to find the
   lowest prisoner number.   Further modify it to also record and
   print the cell number of this prisoner.

Example: Additional arrays can be defined to tell additional facts
   about the prisoners.   The length of sentence and the ages on
   arrival might also be of interest, defined as new arrays A and L,
   for example

Cell	1	2	3	4
Prisoner number	631	127	458	390
Sentence	99	1	53	30
Age on arrival	40	44	35	21

The following part program is used to define these

```
1Ø PRINT "INPUT PRISONER NO. , SENTENCE, AND AGE"
2Ø FOR I=1 TO 4
3Ø INPUT N(I),L(I),A(I)
4Ø NEXT I
```

Problems using this data are found at the end of this Unit.

3 Longer Lists – the DIM statement

In the previous examples the space taken up by a list has been
ignored.   BASIC assumes that a list contains as many as 10 values
and sets space aside for them, and so there is no difficulty as long

as subscripts are smaller than 10.   However it may be necessary to
have a longer list and BASIC allows a program to ask for more room
with the DIM statement.

The DIM statement specifies the size of lists:

line number DIM *name* (*size*), *name* (*size*)...

The *integer size* specifies the largest subscript that will ever be
used by the program for the *list variable name*.   The DIM statement
can appear anywhere in the program.   Like the REM or DEF FN statement, a running program takes no action when it is reached.   It is
simply for the information of BASIC.   Most programmers put it at the
beginning for clarity.   A particular variable name should appear in
only one DIM statement.

Examples:

    5 DIM N(4),L(4),A(4)

reserves 4 spaces for the lists A, L, and N.   This statement could
have appeared in the previous example and would save space.

    63 DIM X7(2ØØ)

reserves 200 spaces for a list called X7.

4 Shuffling Lists

In calculations using scalar variable names, the idea of replacing
one variable by a new value after calculation has occured frequently,
for example in the recurrence relationship of a series evaluation.
The same concept also applies to list calculations, except that the
replacements are often done in some ordered way within the list.   As
an illustration the same prisoners could be required to rotate in
their cells, so that each moves down one cell number, except the
prisoner in cell 1, who moves to cell 4.

In a computer program only one value can be moved at a time;   in
the prison analogy this would correspond to having only one guard to
move the prisoners.   The sequence of operations would be:

The prisoner in cell 1 moves out temporarily.
The old prisoner in cell 2 becomes the new prisoner in cell 1.
The old prisoner in cell 3 becomes the new prisoner in cell 2.
The old prisoner in cell 4 becomes the new prisoner in cell 3.

and finally
The old prisoner in cell 1 becomes the new prisoner in cell 4.

The effect of this reshuffling is:

Before			After	
Cell	Prisoner		Cell	Prisoner
1	631		1	127
2	127		2	458
3	458		3	390
4	390		4	631

If there are other arrays associated with the original order, then
these should also be shuffled. The prisoners moving into cells 1
and 3 would not be happy if they inherited the previous inmate's
sentence.

A program segment which moves the prisoners and keeps track of
their sentences could be:

```
3Ø REM STORE PRISONER FROM CELL 1 TEMPORARILY
4Ø LET X1=N(1)
5Ø LET X2=L(1)
6Ø REM MOVE THE OTHERS DOWN ONE CELL
7Ø FOR I=1 TO 3
8Ø LET N(I)=N(I+1)
9Ø LET L(I)=L(I+1)
1ØØ NEXT I
11Ø REM PUT TEMPORARY PRISONER IN CELL 4
12Ø LET N(4)=X1
13Ø LET L(4)=X2
```

A very common and embarrassing program error arises if the shuffle
is done in the wrong sequence. The prisoners have been moved down
in ascending cell order. If they had been moved down in descending
order, then the old prisoner in cell 4 would be in cells 1, 2, and 3
and it would be some time before the other two were missed. Thus
the shuffle can be performed downwards in ascending order, in which
case the first convict goes into temporary storage. Alternatively
they can be moved upwards in descending order in which case the
temporary storage is used for the last convict.

5 Problems

PROBLEM 10.1   Using the data for prisoner numbers, sentences, and
   ages, write a program to find

   (i) the cell number of the prisoner with the shortest unexpired
        sentence
  (ii) the prisoner number of the oldest prisoner
 (iii) the sentence of the prisoner whose age is closest to the
        mean.

PROBLEM 10.2   In the same jail the policy is to release a prisoner
   for good behaviour when he has either served half his sentence
   rounded up to the nearest year or has reached the age of 70.
   Write a program to determine how many years each will serve
   assuming good behaviour.

PROBLEM 10.3   Write a program which re-arranges the prisoners so
   their cells are organized in

   (i) ascending order of prisoner number

  (ii) descending order of sentence assuming good behaviour as
        defined in Problem 10.2

PROBLEM 10.4   The conversion of numbers from base 10 to another
   base can now be organized properly using a list to hold the
   digits of the result. As before, the digits are found in reverse
   order by the remainders after successive division. Now they can
   be saved in the correct order by placing them backwards in the
   list. Alternatively the list of results could be printed in
   reverse order. Before writing the program work out how long a
   list is needed assuming that the largest decimal number is
   10 000 and the smallest base is 2.

   Example: Find 131 to base 7

   Successive division by 7:   131/7 = 18 remainder 5
                                18/7 = 2 remainder 4
                                 2/7 = 0 remainder 2
   Answer: 245

PROBLEM 10.5   In the Pascal triangle, each number is the sum of the
   two above it. Therefore each row can be generated from the
   previous one - a sort of row by row recurrence. Write a program
   to evaluate and print Pascal's triangle by this method.

UNIT 11
CHARACTER STRINGS

1 Introduction

This unit describes how BASIC can manipulate strings of alphabetic characters. Character string constants have been used as messages in PRINT statements in this course. Now it will be seen that these can be put to several further uses. The string variable facility allows messages to be used in several other statements of BASIC. Some of the more restricted forms of BASIC will allow only a few of the operations described here, and by contrast a few extended versions of BASIC offer a range of string manipulation functions which are not described here.

2 Messages as Constants or Variables

A string constant is any series of acceptable symbols enclosed by quotation marks, and can include letters, numeric digits, blanks, and a number of other characters. The only BASIC symbol not permitted is the quotation mark itself, because it is used to delimit the constant. In the BASIC statement

77 PRINT "THIS IS A STRING CONSTANT"

the message 'THIS IS A STRING CONSTANT' is a string constant.

A string variable is given one of 26 special names which are reserved for this use. These consist of a letter and the dollar sign $. Therefore the names available are

A$, B$, ..., Z$

String variables can be subscripted. Therefore the statement

1Ø DIM A$(75)

defines a string list or array with 75 entries.

3 Using Character Strings in BASIC Statements

Meaningful operations on character strings can be performed by many of the statements of BASIC. The use of string constants in the PRINT statement is familiar, and other uses are outlined here.

(a)   LET

The LET statement may contain a string variable on the left hand side, and a string variable or constant on the right hand side. However string expressions cannot replace ordinary variables and numeric expressions cannot replace string variables. Thus the use of LET with strings is restricted to:

line number LET $\dfrac{string}{variable}$ = $\dfrac{string\ variable}{or\ constant}$

Note, however that subscripted forms are allowed.

Example:

```
1∅ LET A$=B$
2∅ LET C$="MUD IN YOUR EYE"
3∅ LET D$=E$(I+3*J)
4∅ LET F$(L)="YOUR GRANDMOTHER WEARS ARMY BOOTS"
```

(b)   PRINT

The PRINT statement can include either string constants or string variables. The comma and semicolon used as delimiters have the usual meaning.

Example:

```
1∅ LET M$="DISGUSTING"
2∅ PRINT"TODAY'S MESSAGE IS "M$
3∅ END
```

(c)   INPUT

The INPUT statement can include string variables. The message typed in response to the INPUT request does not need quotation marks unless the message contains commas (because the commas would

be confused with the delimiters separating input values). If
quotation marks are used, then different strings do not need commas
to separate them.

EXERCISE   Experiment with

            1∅ INPUT A$,B$
            2∅ PRINT A$;B$
            3∅ END

paying particular attention to the rules for delimiters outlined
above.

    Note that when asking for character input, the command STOP may
not work. The program

            1∅ INPUT A$
            2∅ PRINT A$
            3∅ GO TO 1∅
            4∅ END

could present difficulties. If asking for string input in an endless loop it would be wise to check for the stop message, as

            15 IF A$="STOP" THEN 4∅

See the IF ... THEN statement which follows.

(d)   IF ... THEN

    A very useful application of string variables is in the IF ...
THEN statement. Two strings can be compared as

    line number IF *string* $\begin{array}{c}\textit{relational}\\\textit{operator}\end{array}$ *string* THEN *line number*

for example

            25∅ IF"ABC"<B$(I) THEN 3∅∅

will compare the string constant "ABC" with the list entry B$(I).
If "ABC" is earlier in alphabetical order than B$(I) the jump occurs
to line 300. Thus a string comparison is done on the basis of
alphabetical order - it is not necessary for the strings to be of
the same length, as the following examples show:

```
        "ABC"  is greater than  "ABB"
                          or  "AB"

     "ABC"      is equal to  "ABC"

     "ABC"      is less than  "ABD"
                          or  "ABCA"
                          or  "ABC "   (Note the blank.)
```

Comparison between strings and arithmetic expressions is not recommended.

(e)   DIM

String variables may be used with subscripts and so can form lists. As with ordinary variables, the use must be consistent. If not given explicitly, the maximum size is taken as 10. It will be seen later that arrays can have one, two, or three subscripts and strings are not an exception.

(f)   DATA and READ

These statements are introduced in the next unit and as will be seen they can be used with strings.

4 Problems

PROBLEM 11.1   Write a program which translates integer numbers into their English digits. (Remainders again - use a string array for the words.)

   Example   123 is ONE TWO THREE

PROBLEM 11.2   Write a program which sorts a list into alphabetical order.

PROBLEM 11.3   Write a program to assist an author in preparing an index. He goes through his book at a terminal, typing in the headings and page numbers as they are encountered. When he is finished, he types in 'FINISHED', assuming this message will not occur in his index. The program then sorts his lists according to the alphabetical order of the headings. The same heading may occur several times. The index is then printed with one entry for each heading. If there are repeated entries for a heading, the page numbers appear in order on one line of the output. The author will, of course, further edit this index.

UNIT 12
DEFINING VALUES IN ADVANCE

1 Introduction

Several times in earlier units it was necessary to give a program data values that were known in advance by the laborious method of typing them in whenever the program was run, or through a long series of LET statements. The assignment of sentences and ages to the prisoners in Unit 10 was one example, and in the problems with strings the same difficulty will have arisen. This unit describes the convenient way of setting up data constants in a program once and for all.

2 Assigning Values – the DATA, READ, and RESTORE statements

BASIC allows a list of constants to be set aside in the computer in the DATA statement, and these values can be assigned to any variable using the READ statement. This facility eliminates the need to enter known constants every time a program is run.

The DATA statement has the form:

line number DATA *constant, constant ...*

The DATA statement itself has no effect in a running BASIC program. In this it resembles several other statements encountered earlier including the DIM statement. It is a statement for the information of BASIC, and it causes the constants to be stored in the computer, where they can be retrieved by a READ statement when the program is run. Any number of DATA statements can be included in a program and they can be put anywhere. Their order is important, however. The constants can be numbers in any of the usual BASIC forms, or they can be string constants as will be seen later.

An example of a DATA statement is:

        1∅ DATA 38.2,10.5,-9.6

The READ statement is used to assign values from the DATA

statement to the desired variables.   It is written as

   line number READ *variable,variable*

   This statement is acted upon by a running program.   Values are
assigned to the named variables from the DATA statements in order
and in one-to-one correspondence with the requirements of the READ
statement.   For example, consider the program

```
1Ø DATA 38.2,1Ø.5,-9.6
2Ø READ A,B,C
3Ø PRINT A,B,C
4Ø END
```

In this program, A will be assigned the value 38.2, B the value 10.5,
and C will be -9.6.

   Successive READ statements in the running program carry on through
the DATA list.   Therefore if only part of a DATA statement is used by
a given READ, then the next READ starts with the next value.   In
effect a pointer moves through the DATA constants as values are
requested by READ statements.

   The program

```
1Ø DATA 38.2,1Ø.5,-9.6
2Ø FOR I=1 TO 3
3Ø READ Z
4Ø PRINT Z
5Ø NEXT I
6Ø END
```

Here, the DATA pointer is initially at the beginning of the list:

NEXT VALUE
   ↓
   38.2   1Ø.5   -9.6

When I = 1, the statement READ Z assigns 38.2 to Z and moves the
pointer along:

                        NEXT VALUE
                            ↓
   38.2   1Ø.5   -9.6

so that when I = 2, 10.5 is assigned to Z and the pointer moves again:

NEXT VALUE
↓
38.2   1∅.5   -9.6

and the final request assigns Z to be -9.6.

Similarly, if more variables are requested by one READ statement
than are given by one DATA statement, the next DATA statement
according to line number is taken. Thus the order of DATA statements is important because the DATA area is made up from the DATA
statements taken in order. It is wrong to ask for more constants
than are present in all the DATA statements.

Example:

```
1∅ DATA 38.2
2∅ FOR I=1 TO 3
3∅ DATA 1∅.5
4∅ READ Z
5∅ DATA -9.6
6∅ PRINT Z
7∅ DATA 4E31
8∅ NEXT I
9∅ DATA 75
1∅∅ END
```

This example indicates how the DATA statements can be broken up,
but is also an example of how to make a program hard to read.
This is not good style.

The RESTORE statement returns the pointer to the beginning of
the DATA area, so that all the given data can be re-used. There is
no direct means of returning to the middle of the DATA list, but it
is possible to return to the beginning with RESTORE and read through
to the desired place, for example in a FOR and NEXT loop.

RESTORE has the form:

line number RESTORE

EXERCISE Try the following program:

```
1Ø  DATA  1,2,3
2Ø  FOR  J = 1  TO  2
3Ø  FOR  I = 1  TO  3
4Ø  READ  X
5Ø  PRINT  X;
6Ø  NEXT  I
7Ø  RESTORE
8Ø  NEXT  J
9Ø  END
```

The behaviour of the pointer in this program is then:

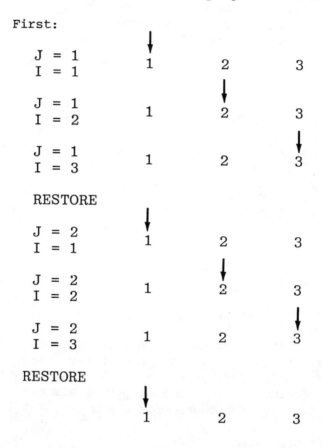

First:

J = 1
I = 1   1   2   3

J = 1
I = 2   1   2   3

J = 1
I = 3   1   2   3

RESTORE

J = 2
I = 1   1   2   3

J = 2
I = 2   1   2   3

J = 2
I = 3   1   2   3

RESTORE

             1   2   3

3 Assigning Values to a List

Values are assigned to a list variable in much the same way as to any other, except that subscripts have to be used. To fill an array from the DATA area, FOR ... NEXT loops must therefore be used.

Examples:

```
1Ø DATA 38.2,1Ø.5,-9.6        1Ø DATA 38.2
2Ø FOR I=1 TO 3               2Ø FOR I=1 TO 3
3Ø READ X(I)                  3Ø DATA 1Ø.5
4Ø NEXT I                     4Ø READ X(I)
5Ø PRINT X(1),X(2),X(3)       5Ø DATA -9.6
6Ø END                        6Ø NEXT I
                              7Ø PRINT X(1),X(2),X(3)
                              8Ø END
```

As before, the second example illustrates the point but is poor style.

4 Assigning Values to String Variables

String constants can be included in DATA statements, for example

   1Ø DATA 1ØØ,STRING,2ØØ,CONSTANT

stores the string constants 'STRING' and 'CONSTANT' in the DATA area alongside the numeric values. As in response to an INPUT statement, no ambiguities are allowed in delimiting the constants of a DATA statement. Therefore quotation marks are required if a comma appears in the string and also if the first symbol in the string would cause confusion with numeric values; the confusing ones are space, digit, plus, minus, or decimal point.

Examples:

   1Ø DATA STRING,CONSTANT

defines two string constants 'STRING' and 'CONSTANT'

   1Ø DATA"STRING,CONSTANT"

defines one string constant 'STRING,CONSTANT' which includes a comma

   3Ø DATA "+FIVE"," GO","...AND THEN","123 ZOOM"

defines a number of string constants which require the quotation marks.

The READ statement can obviously include string variable names which must correspond in position with string constants in the DATA list.

Examples:

```
1Ø DATA 1ØØ,STRING,2ØØ,CONSTANT
2Ø READ X,A$,Y,B$
3Ø PRINT A$;B$
4Ø END
```

5 Problems

PROBLEM 12.1   Looking up an entry in a table is a very common
requirement, especially in the commercial world. Establish a
list of numbers by a DATA statement and make a program to search
the list for a particular entry that may or may not appear.

PROBLEM 12.2 Write a program to translate an integer into English
digits. This time the digits can be stored in a DATA area. E.g.
123 is ONE TWO THREE.

PROBLEM 12.3 A company payroll is defined in DATA statements. The
first one tells how many employees there are. There is then one
further statement for each employee defining among other things
their name and salary. Write a program to read the list which
is in no particular order, and print two summaries, one in
alphabetical order and the other in reverse order of earnings.
If you feel ambitious tax them heavily for all kinds of things
and print their miserably small monthly cheques.

PROBLEM 12.4 The solution to problem 12.1 will have involved
searching the list entirely each time. A "binary search" is much
more efficient. Suppose there is a jail with 16 prisoners in it.
Define their cell numbers, ages and sentences in order of
prisoner number. Write a program which enables the Warden to
type in a prisoner number and retrieve the information about
the prisoner and his probable real sentence for good behaviour
as defined in problem 10.2. Do this by a 'binary search'. First
the prisoner number is compared with the number 8 in the list to
find which half it is in (or it might by luck be the eighth).
Then it is compared with number 4 or number 12 to find which
quarter it is in, and so on. For example if prisoner number 53
was the third in the list the program would decide on first half,
first quarter, second eighth and finally find him. In a 16
prisoner jail it can never take more than 4 tries to locate a
prisoner.

UNIT 13
SUBROUTINES

1 Introduction

Properly used, the subroutine is another facility which can improve the structure of a program. With the function definition statement described in Unit 9, a one line calculation could be expressed as a function and then referred to throughout a program. With subroutines, a computation of any length and complexity can be written as a separate unit and then used at will in a program.

2 Defining Subroutines – the GOSUB and RETURN statements

A subroutine is a separate program module not restricted to one line which is written as a self-contained unit, starting at some line number which does not occur elsewhere, and containing its own line numbers in order. The program calls for the subroutine explicitly in a GOSUB statement, and to get back from the subroutine the RETURN statement is necessary.

Example: A subroutine is required to evaluate the factorial of a number. Suppose N9 is a positive integer or zero, and its factorial is required. The factorial of N9 is the product of all the integers from 1 to N9 and the factorial of zero is 1. A subroutine is written starting at line 2000 to work out this product in a FOR...NEXT loop:

```
2000 REM SUBROUTINE TO FIND FACTORIAL OF N9
2010 REM ANSWER IN N8, I9 IS USED
2020 LET N8=1
2030 FOR I9=2 TO N9
2040 LET N8=N8*I9
2050 NEXT I9
2060 RETURN
2070 END
```

This subroutine always finds the factorial of N9 and returns the answer as N8. Variable I9 is used in the calculation. To use this subroutine as part of a BASIC program care must be taken that I9, N8, and N9 are not used in a conflicting way because the same variables are shared by all parts of the program.

A program to make use of this subroutine could be:

```
1Ø REM THIS IS A PROGRAM TO FIND FACTORIALS
2Ø REM OF NUMBERS TYPED INTO THE TERMINAL
3Ø REM
4Ø REM REQUEST INPUT
5Ø PRINT "NUMBER WHOSE FACTORIAL IS REQUIRED";
6Ø INPUT N9
7Ø GOSUB 2ØØØ
8Ø PRINT "FACTORIAL" N9 "IS" N8
9Ø GO TO 5Ø
```

When these are used together, the subroutine is called at line 70 by the GOSUB statement. On its completion at line 2060, the subroutine comes back with the RETURN statement.

The power of the subroutine lies in its ability to return to the place from which it was called. It could be called from a program several times, or from another subroutine or both. However it is obviously that neither should one subroutine call itself, nor should an endless loop of subroutines be established.

EXERCISE   Run this program. Notice the semicolon in line 50.

The statements provided for subroutine usage are:

line number a GOSUB *line number b*

This statement causes a jump to a subroutine at *line number b*.

line number   RETURN

This statement sends the program back to the line following the GOSUB which called it.

3 Terminating Programs – the STOP statement

Before subroutines were introduced, the END statement was sufficient both to end and terminate a program. The END statement is still required to be the highest numbered line in a BASIC program, subroutines and all. Therefore a program must always end with one and only one END statement. Even with subroutines present, it still could be used to terminate the running of a program by jumping there with a GO TO. However the STOP statement is available to stop or terminate the running of a program and can be put anywhere in the program.   It is simply:

  line number STOP

and when it is encountered, execution of the program stops.   Thus in the example of section 2, line 90 could have been a STOP statement.

4 An Example

A program to find the area under a curve is the kind of requirement which is suitable for organization as a subroutine.   The algorithm is easily separated in any program which will use it, and it is likely that a good one would be useful to many people.

The trapezoidal rule which was illustrated in Fig. 7.2, is a simple method for finding the area under a curve.   The area of the shaded trapezoid was

$$\text{area} = \frac{f(x_1) + f(x_2)}{2} (x_2 - x_1)$$

If a larger number of trapezoids are taken, then the area is obtained by summation.   In Fig. 13.1 a curve has been divided into N9 trapezoids between X8 and X9, and here

$$\text{area} = H9*\left\{ \frac{f(X8) + f(X9)}{2} + f(X8+H9) + f(X8+2*H9) \right.$$
$$\left. + \ldots + f(X8+(N9-1)*H9) \right\}$$

where $H9 = \dfrac{X9 - X8}{N9}$

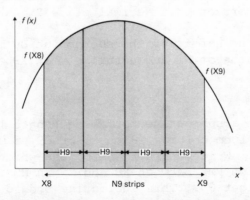

Fig. 13.1. Illustrating the trapezoidal rule with many segments.

A BASIC subroutine which finds the area under a curve which is defined by FNZ(X) between limits X8 and X9 using N9 strips is given below. To use this, it is necessary to define the function FNZ and call the subroutine with the desired values of X8, X9 and N9 already assigned. The subroutine makes use of the variable S9 for summation, I9 for counting, and H9 for the strip width. The subroutine assumes correct values of X8, X9, and N9 and will work for any integer N9 greater than 0.

```
6000 REM AREA UNDER A CURVE FNZ BY TRAPEZOID RULE
6010 REM FROM X8 TO X9 IN N9 STRIPS
6020 REM VARIABLES S9, I9, AND H9 ARE USED
6030 REM
6040 REM CALCULATE STRIP WIDTH
6050 LET H9=(X9-X8)/N9
6060 REM END VALUES OF SUM
6070 LET S9=0.5*(FNZ(X8)+FNZ(X9))
6080 REM DO REMAINING SUM
6090 FOR I9=N9-1 TO 1 STEP -1
6100 LET S9=S9+FNZ(X8+I9*H9)
6110 NEXT I9
6120 REM MULTIPLY BY H9 AND RETURN
6130 LET S9=S9*H9
6140 RETURN
```

EXERCISE   Write a program to use this subroutine which accepts X8, X9, and N9 in an INPUT statement and find the area under

$$\frac{1}{\sqrt{2\pi}}\, e^{-x^2/2}$$

between $x = 0$ and $x = 1$. How many strips are required to give an answer which is correct to 4 decimal places?

EXERCISE   Improve the safety of the subroutine by making it check for a sensible value of N9 and ensuring that X9 > X8.

5 Problems

PROBLEM 13.1   Write a subroutine to make a single line of a bar graph by shading from columns C8 to C9 or C9 to C8 depending on which is greater. Write another subroutine which draws a bar graph of a function FNX between X8 and X9 in N9 steps using scale factor K9 and offset 09. This subroutine should call on the first one to do the actual drawing. Using these draw a shaded graph of a cosine.

PROBLEM 13.2   Write a subroutine which scans the first L9 entries in a list Q9, and finds the largest value M9 and its position N9.

PROBLEM 13.3   Write a subroutine which sorts a string list A$ of length L9 into alphabetical order.

PROBLEM 13.4   Write a subroutine to solve the equation

$$FNY(X) = 0$$

by Newton's method given the initial guess X9. The subroutine should return the answer R9 when the latest step size is less than E9.   Use this to find the square root of 2.

PROBLEM 13.5   Another method of area calculation is known as Simpson's rule, Fig. 13.2. Here two adjoining segments are fitted by a parabolic curve and the shaded area a is

$$a = \frac{h}{3}\left\{f(x_1) + 4f(x_2) + f(x_3)\right\}$$

Write a subroutine to divide the range from X8 to X9 of a function FNZ into 2*N9 strips and find the area by Simpson's rule.   Using this calculate the area under

$$f(x) = \frac{1}{\sqrt{2\pi}}\,e^{-x^2/2}$$

between $x = 0$ and $x = 1$ and find out how many strips are required for 4 decimal places of accuracy.   How does the number required compare with the trapezoidal rule?

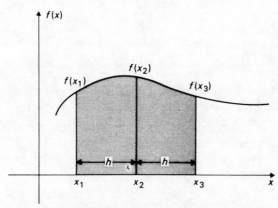

Fig. 13.2. Illustrating Simpson's rule.

UNIT 14
WORKING WITH TABLES

1 Introduction

The concept of a list was introduced in Unit 10, and once the basic idea of using subscripts has been mastered, it is possible to move on to arrays with two subscripts which in BASIC are usually called tables. These are of great importance in computation. Programmers sometimes find that dealing with two subscripts does not come easily, so a careful approach to this unit is advisable.

2 Tables and Subscripts

BASIC in fact provides for arrays of up to three subscripts. It has already been seen that with one subscript a list is formed, such as

$$A(1)$$
$$A(2)$$
$$A(3)$$

The extension to two subscripts is straightforward enough. A variable with two subscripts forms a table, such as

$$C(1,1) \quad C(1,2) \quad C(1,3)$$
$$C(2,1) \quad C(2,2) \quad C(2,3)$$
$$C(3,1) \quad C(3,2) \quad C(3,3)$$

Thw BASIC respresentation includes both subscripts, separated by a comma. The order of the subscripts should be noted; the first gives the row number and the second is the column number.

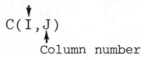

Row number
$$C(I,J)$$
Column number

In a similar way it is possible to use three subscripts, which is the maximum allowed in BASIC.

Any variable which is used with subscripts is automatically recognized by BASIC to be an array. Now that both lists and tables are available it is necessary to be consistent in a program about the number of subscripts used with variable names. Once a list, always a list. Once a table, always a table. If no DIM statement is given, the largest possible subscript is taken to be 10. The form of the DIM statement should be generalized slightly:

$$\textit{line number} \text{ DIM } \textit{variable} \left(\begin{array}{c} \textit{up to three} \\ \textit{integer sizes,} \\ \textit{commas between} \end{array} \right), \textit{variable} \left(\begin{array}{c} \textit{up to three} \\ \textit{integer sizes,} \\ \textit{commas between} \end{array} \right) \ldots$$

The *variable* can be a string variable or an ordinary variable.

Example:

        3Ø DIM Q$(23),Z(25,4Ø)

defines a string list Q$ with up to 23 entries and an ordinary table Z with 25 rows and 40 columns.

3 Calculating with Tables

Lists and tables are dealt with in much the same way, but in working with tables the demands on the thought processes can be more severe in keeping track of the rows and columns.

Suppose a company has four products and four branch offices. A record of sales figures for a particular quarter is kept in table form:

Containers Ltd

		Branch			
		London	Manchester	Liverpool	Birmingham
	Bottles	43	96	51	331
Product	Bags	600	143	270	201
	Boxes	215	400	311	192
	Bibelots	307	351	492	331

In a BASIC program DATA statements could be used to store the names of the cities and the products and also to save the table of values:

```
1Ø DATA  43,96,51,331
2Ø DATA  6ØØ,143,27Ø,2Ø1
3Ø DATA  215,4ØØ,311,192
4Ø DATA  3Ø7,351,492,331
5Ø DATA  LONDON,MANCHESTER,LIVERPOOL,BIRMINGHAM
6Ø DATA  BOTTLES,BAGS,BOXES,BIBELOTS
```

For convenience each row is written in one DATA statement, although there is nothing wrong with compressing the information into fewer statements.   The data can be read into the table T in the following way:

```
1ØØ FOR I=1 TO 4
11Ø FOR J=1 TO 4
12Ø READ T(I,J)
13Ø NEXT J
14Ø NEXT I
```

Note carefully that the data has been read across the row by making the column number J increase most rapidly.   I and J are popular variables to use as row and column numbers.

It is known from earlier work how string lists can be set up:

```
17Ø FOR K=1 TO 4
18Ø READ A$(K)
190 NEXT K
2ØØ FOR K=1 TO 4
21Ø READ B$(K)
22Ø NEXT K
```

After this has been done, A$ has the city names corresponding to the columns.   B$ on the other hand is different from the others because it is organized to coincide with the rows and this will be important later.

Now that the table has been set up it can be calculated in various ways.   First of all the rows are inspected to see how each commodity fares in the various cities.   For each product the total sales and the best city are found:

```
300 FOR I=1 TO 4
310 LET S=0
320 LET M=0
330 FOR J=1 TO 4
340 LET S=S+T(I,J)
350 IF T(I,J)<M THEN 370
360 LET M=T(I,J)
370 LET M$=A$(J)
380 NEXT J
390 PRINT"WE HAVE SOLD"S;B$(I);
400 PRINT"WE DID BEST IN"M$"WHERE WE SOLD"M;B$(I)
410 NEXT I
```

EXERCISE   Put this program together and run it.   Improve the
   presentation.

4 Problems

PROBLEM 14.1   All the products of Containers Ltd. are sold in cases
   of value £1, and the data given are in cases.   Process the columns
   to find out the total sales for each city and which product sold
   best in that city.

PROBLEM 14.2   Shuffle the table of Containers Ltd by program so
   that the cities and products are in alphabetical order.   Print
   the table with headings in this form.

PROBLEM 14.3   Shuffle the table by program so that the cities are
   in order of greatest total sales there and the products are also
   in order of greatest total sales in all cities.   Print the table
   with headings in this form.

PROBLEM 14.4   Write a story writing program using a table in which
   column 1 is an adjective, column 2 is a noun, column 3 a verb,
   column 4 an adverb, column 5 another adjective and column 6 a
   noun.   Ask 6 friends to each type in 10 words to fill one
   column without consulting the others.   Print the story.   Then
   shuffle each column into alphabetical order and print this as
   Chapter 2.   Some people have used computers to write music in a
   similar fashion - it too is sometimes pretty funny.

APPENDIX
A SUMMARY OF BASIC BASIC

This summary describes a universal subset of BASIC. Some systems will support facilities not described here, including additional commands, additional functions, and file manipulation statements.

1 BASIC Programs

A program in BASIC consists of numbered statements, or lines, of the form

line number statement

Example:
```
10 PRINT 5/7
20 END
```

When a BASIC program is executed, using the command RUN, the statements are obeyed in order of their line numbers unless the program itself dictates otherwise. The last line of every BASIC program must be an END statement.

2 Commands

Every BASIC system should support at least the following three commands, or some equivalent:

(i)   RUN - the current BASIC program is executed
(ii) LIST - the current BASIC program is printed on the terminal
(iii) NEW - the current BASIC program is lost so that a new one
            may be commenced.

3 Creating BASIC Programs

All keyboard entries to the BASIC system, except when a program is running, will be interpreted as statements if the line begins with a number. Otherwise they will be interpreted as commands.

(a)   Entering - programs are entered by typing each line with a
      line number and ending with the 'carriage return' key.
      (Unit 1)

(b)   Correcting - a line is replaced by typing the replacement in full, including the line number and the 'carriage return' key.   (Unit 1)

(c)   Correcting lines while typing - the symbol ← ('back arrow') or _ ('underline') eliminates the character before it. (Unit 1)

(d)   Inserting - a new line is inserted between two others by the use of a suitable line number.   (Unit 1)

(e)   Deleting - a line is deleted by typing the line number and 'carriage return'. (Unit 1)

4 Numbers in BASIC

Numbers in BASIC can be expressed in three forms:

(a)   Integers - a number written without a decimal point, e.g. 123

(b)   A number written with a decimal point, e.g. 3.1416

(c)   Exponential - a number written with an exponential indicated by the letter E, e.g. 1E10 means 1×10^{10}.   (Unit 3)

5 Variables in BASIC

(a)   Ordinary variables which represent numeric values in BASIC can be assigned any of 286 names which are the single letters:

$$A, B, C, \ldots Z$$

or any letter plus a single digit:

$$A0, A1, \ldots A9$$
$$B0, B1, \ldots B9$$
$$Z0, Z1, \ldots Z9 \qquad \text{(Unit 3)}$$

(b)   Most BASIC systems allow string variables which are identified by the 26 names:

$$A\$, B\$, \ldots Z\$ \qquad \text{(Unit 11)}$$

(c)   Scalars
A variable is scalar if it is written without a subscript in which case it represents a single value, e.g. X7.

(d)   Arrays
A variable is an array or list if it is written with up to three subscripts, in which case it represents a list of values, e.g. Q\$(9),N(I,J),T(1,2,3).   An array must always have the same number of subscripts.   (Units 10 and 14)

(e)   Subscripts
A subscript can be any arithmetic expression, however the
resulting value must be between 1 and the maximum array size.
Non-integer subscripts are truncated to integers.   (Unit 10)

(f)   Array sizes
The maximum size of an array is set up by the DIM statement,
or by default to 10 in each subscript if no DIM statement is
given.   (Unit 10)

6 Character String Constants

(a)   String constants are sequences of symbols usually enclosed
in quotation marks, e.g. 'HELLO SAILOR'.   They may be used
in the PRINT statement (Unit 1).   Some systems may allow
their use in DATA, IF...THEN, and on the right hand side of
the LET statement.   (Unit 11)

(b)   String variables have the 26 variable names are A$, B$,...Z$.
They may be used in the statements INPUT, PRINT, READ,
IF...THEN, LET and DIM (and so may be subscripted).   (Unit
11)

(c)   In comparing the strings using the IF...THEN statement, strings
nearer the beginning of the alphabet are less than those nearer
the end.   (Unit 11)

e.g.   "AB" is less than "AC"
            "AB" is less than "ABA"

7 Arithmetic Expressions

BASIC arithmetic uses the hierarchy of operators

	( )	expressions in brackets	high priority
	↑	exponentiation	
operators	* /	multiplication and division	
	+ -	addition and subtraction	low priority

Operations of equal priority are performed from left to right.
Arithmetic expressions may be written involving these operations and
any variables or constants, e.g. (A+3)/D(I).

A single variable or constant is itself a valid expression.

Two operators may not appear together, e.g. A+-B is not allowed.
Operators normally separate two values, e.g. 3*B, but the
operator - has 'unary' meaning, e.g. -J or 3*(-B).   (Unit 2)

8 Relational Expressions

(a)   Relational expressions are written

| arithmetic expression | relational operator | arithmetic expression |

e.g. A > B

The result of a relational expression is TRUE or FALSE.
Relational expressions are used in the IF...THEN statement.
(Unit 5)

(b)   The available relational operators are

```
          =        equal to
          >        greater than
          <        less than
  > = or => greater or equal
  < = or =< less or equal
  < > or >< not equal                    (Unit 5)
```

(c)   In some systems relational expressions can be more complicated
involving the additional operations AND and OR (inclusive) as in

$$(A<B*1\emptyset)OR(C>=1)$$

(d)   In some systems the results TRUE or FALSE have the values 1
and 0 and can be used as part of any arithmetic expression.
(e)   In some systems the string relational expression is
available:

| string | relational operator | string |

e.g. "ABC">=B$(I)

9 Library Functions

All BASIC systems should support the following set of library
functions:

Function	Meaning
SIN(x)	The sine of x where x is an angle in radians
COS(x)	The cosine of x where x is in radians
TAN(x)	The tangent of x where x is in radians
ATN(x)	The arctangent of an angle x in the range $-\pi/2$ to $+\pi/2$ radians

EXP(x)	The value of e^x
LOG(x)	The natural logarithm of x
ABS(x)	The absolute value of x
SQR(x)	The square root of x
INT(x)	The largest integer not greater than x.
	Example INT(5.95)=5 and INT(-5.95)=-6.
SGN(x)	The sign of x, has value 1 if x is positive; 0 if x
	is 0; or -1 if x is negative.

In the above functions, x represents any expression which may
of course include other functions. The quantity x is called the
argument or parameter of the function. (Unit 6)

A function RND, which is a random number generator, appears in
most versions of BASIC. It does not always have an argument - if
it does, the argument may not have a meaning.

The TAB function is a special function associated with the PRINT
statement, as described in section 11 of this appendix.

10   The Statements of Basic BASIC

The statements of BASIC are summarized here in alphabetical order.
Items in square brackets are optional.

line number DATA *constant, constant* ...

> The *constants* given in the DATA statement are stored in the
> computer in the order given. Successive DATA statements add to
> the list in order. Information from the list is assigned to
> variables by the READ statement. (Unit 12)
> Some systems allow strings to be defined in the DATA statement,
> and the quotation marks can be left out if the string does not
> contain blanks, plus signs, digits, minus signs, decimal points,
> or commas.

> E.g.   DATA STRING,"STRING+31"   (Unit 11)

line number DEF FN*a* (*variable*) = *expression*

> This statement is used for function definition. See section 12
> of this appendix.   (Unit 9)

line number DIM *subscripted variable, subscripted variable* ...

> The DIM statement specifies the maximum size of arrays. In the
> DIM statement the subscripts must be integer numbers. If an

array is not mentioned in a DIM statement, the maximum is 10 in each subscript.   (Unit 10)

line number END

The END statement must be the last in any BASIC programs, i.e. it must be present and have the highest line number.   When it is encountered the execution of a BASIC program terminates.
(Unit 1)

To terminate a program before the highest line number, the STOP statement is used.   (Unit 13)

line number FOR *variable* = *expression a* TO *expression b* [STEP *expression c*]

The FOR statement begins a FOR...NEXT program loop, which is repeated with the named variable having the initial value given by *expression a* and changing by *expression c* until *expression b* is reached.   The word STEP and *expression c* are optional, and if not given the requirement is taken as 1.   The named *variable* can be adjusted during the loop, but the initial, final, and step values are fixed when the loop first begins and cannot later be changed.   With care, a program can jump out of and into loops. The end of a loop is indicated by a NEXT statement, which must be present.   FOR...NEXT loops using different *variables* may be nested.   (Unit 7)

line number a GOSUB *line number b*

This statement is used to call a subroutine.   See section 12 of this appendix.   (Unit 13)

line number a GO TO *line number b*

The GO TO statement causes a jump to *line number b*.   (Unit 4)

line number a IF *relational expression* THEN *line number b*

When the IF statement is encountered, the *relational expression* is evaluated and if it is TRUE, then the program jumps to *line number b*.   If the *relational expression* is FALSE, the execution continues from the next line after *line number a*.   (Unit 5)

line number INPUT *variable, variable*

The INPUT statement causes the computer to request information

by typing the symbol ?, and waiting until a line of information
is entered.
Exactly the correct number of quantities should be entered,
separated by commas. If too few are entered an explanatory
message is given and the missing information should be typed in.
If too many are entered a different explanatory message appears
and it will be necessary to type all the information again from
the beginning.   (Unit 3)

line number LET *variable = expression*

In the LET statement the expression on the right hand side is
evaluated and the result replaces the value of the variable on
the left hand side.   (Unit 3)

line number NEXT *variable*

The NEXT statement identifies the end of the FOR...NEXT loop in
which the variable was the one used in the FOR statement.
(Unit 7)

line number a ON *expression* GO TO *line number b, line number c,...*

The ON...GO TO statement allows a multiple choice of branches to
the destinations given in *line number b, line number c, ...*
The *expression* is evaluated and truncated to an integer. If the
result is 1, the program jumps to *line number b,* if 2 to *line
number c,* etc. If the *expression* is negative, zero, or too
large for the number of destinations given, an error message is
produced.   (Unit 5)

line number PRINT *quantity delimiter quantity* ...

This statement produces printed output.   See section 11 of this
appendix.

line number READ *variable, variable* ...

The READ statement assigns values to the named *variables* from
the list defined by DATA statements. As successive READ statements are encountered, they continue through the DATA list. In
some systems the *variables* may be string variables.   (Unit 12)

line number REM *any remark or comment*

The REM statement has no effect on the execution of a BASIC

program, and is provided to allow remarks to be inserted to explain the program.   (Unit 3)

line number RESTORE

The RESTORE statement returns subsequent READ statements to the beginning of the DATA list.   (Unit 12)

line number RETURN

This statement is used in subroutines.   See section 12 of this appendix.   (Unit 13)

line number STOP

This statement terminates the execution of a program and is used when a program is to stop before the last line (which is the END statement.)   (Unit 13)

11 Printing

All BASIC systems support the PRINT statement:

line number PRINT *quantity delimiter quantity delimiter...*

where *quantity* can be

(a)   an expression resulting in numerical output
(b)   a character string in quotation marks resulting in literal output
(c)   on some systems, a string variable resulting in literal output
(d)   the TAB function

and *delimiter* can be a comma or semicolon, and can sometimes be omitted as explained below.

A PRINT statement starts a new line unless a final *delimiter* was explicitly given in the previous PRINT, in which case it continues on the same line.
A PRINT statement containing too many *delimiters* for a single printed line will be continued on the following line.

The comma

The print line is divided into 5 zones of 15 spaces.
The comma causes the next *quantity* to be printed beginning in

the first space of the next zone.

The semicolon

between *quantities* causes the output to be compressed.   After a
TAB function or a character string printing continues in the next
space.   Between numerical output the spacing depends on the
numbers (see (d)), for example the field width for small integers
is 6 spaces.   At the end of a print statement the semicolon causes
the next print statement to continue on the same line.

Numbers

may appear in the printed output as integers, or as numbers with
decimal places, or in exponential format.

Character strings

The quotation marks surrounding character strings enable the
delimiter to be left out, in which case a semicolon is assumed,
except at the end of a PRINT statement where the absence of a
delimiter causes the next PRINT statement to start a new line.

The TAB function

TAB(*expression*) may appear as a *quantity* in a PRINT statement.
This causes the printer to move forward to the column number given
by the integer part of the *expression*.   The *expression* must
specify a column number which exists, and the printer cannot move
backwards.

12   Functions and Subroutines

(a)   Functions   (Unit 9)

All BASIC systems support the single line function:

line number DEF FNa (*variable*) = *expression*

a can be the letters A through Z, thus the 26 names, FNA, FNB,...
FNZ are available.

When a function name is implicitly used in a running program, the
expression on the right hand side is evaluated using the given
value of the function *variable*.   The function *variable* is thus a
'dummy' for the value used while running.

Only one definition of a particular function should be used. Functions may use other functions, but endless loops may not be so established.

(b)   Subroutines   (Unit 13)

Subroutines are called by the GOSUB statement:

line number a GOSUB *line number b*

The running program continues from *line number b* until a RETURN is encountered, when it carries on from the line after *line number a*. Subroutines may call other subroutines, but endless loops may not be so established.

Subroutines are ended by the RETURN statement:

line number RETURN

The running program returns to the line after the latest GOSUB.

The STOP statement terminates program execution:

line number STOP

INDEX